HOW TO RUN A RESTAURANT

JOHN McKENNA

HOW TO
run a restaurant

John McKenna

ESTRAGON PRESS

FIRST PUBLISHED IN 1998 BY ESTRAGON PRESS, DURRUS, COUNTY CORK

REPRINTED 1998

THIS EDITION PUBLISHED IN 2004

© ESTRAGON PRESS LTD, 2004

TEXT © JOHN McKENNA

ISBN 1 874076 55 3

PRINTED IN SPAIN BY GRAPHYCEMS

PUBLISHING EDITOR: SALLY McKENNA

DESIGN: NICK CANN

EDITOR: JUDITH CASEY

COVER PHOTOGRAPHY: MIKE O'TOOLE

WEB: FLUIDEDGE

www.bridgestoneguides.com

FOR MAEVE BRACKEN

with thanks to:

turlough mcnamara & jenny mcnally, tom o'connell, ben gorman, jonathan davis, mercy fenton, ross lewis, paul flynn, susan holland & ian parr, otto kunze, bridget healy, simon pratt, leylie hayes, teresa byrne, caroline workman, harry mckeogh

and

yoichi hoashi, frank mckevitt, gary joyce, michael o'rourke, mike o'toole, nick cann, judith casey, chris carroll, josette cadoret, hugh stancliffe, miguel sancho

Contents

"The mealtime service in restaurants has theatrical overtones. The cook makes preparations as best as he or she can and hopes that everyone will really enjoy the food... Tension rises, but also a euphoria that may switch quite quickly to anger if things go badly. What a good psychiatrist would make of it all, I'm not sure."

SHAUN HILL

INTRODUCTION

There are two types of people in the world: those who have worked in restaurants, and those who haven't.

The folk who have had the good fortune to work in restaurants are distinguished from their fellow citizens by having the ability to do six things simultaneously. Those who haven't worked in restaurants do things one at a time, sequentially.

It is this ability amongst people working in the business of food and hospitality to be almost super-human that fascinates me about restaurants, and especially the people who create them.

To understand just what gets done in a busy restaurant, just set yourself the task of programming a computer to do the following actions: over the course of a day, move a small army of people, many of whom barely know one another or know anything about one another, around a series of rooms, working with variable and occasionally very dangerous circumstances – fire; heat; bottles of liquid that virtually explode when you open them (the bubbly), in the presence of colliding objects (the other staff members), with an objective that is designed to deliver an enormous series of logistical conclusions (the lunch and dinner plates) to a huge number of end users (the diners), whose demands are variable at any given time, and whose behaviour is at any given moment of the task, unpredictable – such as the couple who have just had a blazing row.

Is there a computer that could be made to do such a thing? Of course there isn't. Only humans can do this and, of course, many humans cannot do this: so for every restaurateur enthralled by the heat of the kitchen and the action of the dining room, there are a dozen more who can't stand the heat.

This book is for those who are enthralled by, most likely

almost addicted to, the heat and the action that is the *modus operandi* of a restaurant. The book is designed to help people – whether they be students, practitioners or dreamers – to better understand some of the more amorphous, but unquestionably vital, factors that contribute to a restaurant's success.

Restaurants fail most often not because they don't get the figures right, or because they haven't got HACCP clearance or staff working permits, but because they neglect the almost unquantifiable elements that make people want to socialise in a particular room in the first place.

Issues such as design, mood, music, attitude, indeed the very question of exactly why you want to open a restaurant in the first place, are some of the things that restaurateurs most commonly neglect. They seem to imagine that the key elements of attraction for a restaurant audience – comfort, ambience, a signature style in service and cooking – arrive in out of the ether once you have put a few tables and chairs together and written a menu. If only running a restaurant were that simple!

It's not that simple. Running a restaurant requires the ability to do six things at any – and probably every – given moment. And, in addition, requires experience across a broad range of fields. You cannot arrive at the destination which this book aims at – a restaurant with a signature style of cooking, service and ambience – unless you know how to concoct an entire series of happenings in your restaurant. Restaurateurs are renaissance people, and only practical, hands-on, hard-won experience can equip you with an array of skills from design to accountancy, and from diplomacy to how to make the best Bloody Mary in the business.

INTRODUCTION

It is for this reason that the book doesn't tell you about going to catering college, or studying for a degree in the culinary arts, or taking an intensive cookery course, and then sourcing the right building in the right place, and working out pricing schemes and staff wages and so – endlessly – on.

The book doesn't deal with these for the simple reason that they are always variable. If someone tells you that they can work out an exact schema for running your business successfully, don't believe them. For what will work in one place for one audience will fail in another place with a different audience. Restaurants, like every great entertainment, are endlessly diverse and different. That is why we like them.

So, what is the surest way to success? It is to create and maintain a signature style that is yours alone, what the retailers call a USP: a Unique Selling Point. A big brasserie seating 300 people can have a signature style, and so can a little café with a pair of tables. The signatures will be different, and that is what people like, and what people want.

The book also begins on the presumption that restaurants are living in a time of intense and rapid change, and that one of the many skills the restaurateur must acquire is the ability to read the future, to see what the audience will want, and the way in which they will want it. If you stand still, the chances are you will get left behind. There are no fixed rules any longer in the business, no fail-safe mantras: everything is fickle.

What is not fickle is this: people love restaurants. They love the drama, the theatre, the entertainment, the sociability, the sheer sexiness of so much dynamic human interaction.

They also love to eat well, but eating is only one element of a successful restaurant. Indeed, what is noticeable about the testimonies of the restaurateurs quoted in this book, in comparison to their colleagues who kindly gave their opinion in the first edition, is the realisation by so many of them that you will not succeed simply by having very fine cooking. The food itself is not enough.

The age of worshipping chefs, of making pilgrimages to the temples of gastronomy, are over. The prima donna soprano cannot make an operatic production a success all on her own. Ronaldo is nothing without the rest of the Brazilian team to supply him with goal-scoring chances. Jonny Wilkinson needs good feed before that drop kick splits the posts.

The same is true of restaurants. The chef is just one player in the team, and he is not any more important a player than anyone else. From plongeur to payroll clerk, everyone has to be playing the one way, supporting each other, creating chances to win, making beautiful music together.

JOHN McKENNA
DURRUS, COUNTY CORK, JANUARY 2004

1

1

"In countries that don't have a rich inherited cuisine, the growth of good restaurants and cuisine has been partly achieved by people with dreams of one day opening a little restaurant somewhere."

RICK STEIN

THE FUTURE OF RESTAURANTS

Restaurants used to be predictable places that did predictable things, and they used to be places where people behaved predictably.

People used to expect to eat lunch and dinner in restaurants, and they used to do it at set times: between noon and 2pm for lunch, with dinner at varying times from 6.30pm or so onwards. On the seventh day, restaurants rested.

Those days are gone, mainly because people's behaviour has changed for a zillion different reasons. But, many restaurants don't seem to have picked up on this. They don't seem to have cottoned on to the fact that, for instance, people may want to eat restaurant food, but might not want to eat it in the restaurant, so the restaurant offers no take-away or freezer offer for someone who just wants to pick up dinner on their way home from work.

Restaurants often don't seem to realise that they could create a whole new offer if they used their stoves and ovens non-stop, rather than blasting them up to speed for a few hours each morning and evening. If you are baking bread, it is as easy to double the quantity and to sell the surplus to customers or to a retail shop. The same should be true of virtually everything the restaurant cooks: if you can plate it, then you can place it in a plastic tub and retail it.

Restaurants are also places ideally suited to selling choice deli foods they don't make themselves – estate olive oils, olives, piquillo peppers, select grades of tuna and anchovies, wines and beers, you name it.

But very few restaurants do this, even though there are examples here and there of how successful it can be, and how easily it can be done.

THE FUTURE OF RESTAURANTS
time • space • choice

In Fishy Fishy Café, a little fish restaurant and shop in Kinsale, West Cork, Martin and Marie Shanahan cook lunch between about 11.30am and 4pm each day. Even though Kinsale is a resort town, they stay open all year, and have customers all year. But, in addition to cooking some of the finest fish dishes you can eat, they also sell deli foods and, more importantly, they sell cooked fish dinners to be taken away as well as the wet fish they cook.

It is common to see customers in Fishy Fishy walk to the counter after lunch, and choose either some fillets of fish, or else a few portions of the prepared fish dinners. They may very well also pluck something else out of the freezer, and grab something off the shelf, and, hey presto!, their spend has suddenly doubled. They have used Fishy Fishy both as shop and restaurant. They have got what they want. And isn't that what restaurants are supposed to be all about?

Maybe restaurants should be in the business of giving their customers what they want, but it seems to me that many places haven't grasped this idea yet. Too many restaurants continue to give customers only what the restaurant wants to offer, at the times the restaurant wants to offer it.

Despite the evidence of flexible working hours which means people's dining times become infinitely variable, despite the evidence of the CCTT (can't cook, too tired) and the CCNT (can't cook, never tried) classes who dominate our cities and who would just love something decent to eat for dinner after a long day, restaurants still insist that you should sit down at a time that suits them and do things their way. Restaurants still insist on being formal, yet lifestyles today are no longer formal;

they are flexible, and that is what restaurants should be: flexible.

In a provocative and thoughtful article in *The Financial Times*, published in August 2003, the restaurant writer – and former restaurateur – Nicholas Lander asserts that restaurateurs must realise that "the rules governing their profession for the last 200 years no longer apply". Lander quotes Drew Harri, a New Zealander who runs the self-service restaurant, Cosi, in Paris's sixth arrondissement. Harri tells it like this: "No one seems to have any time...you also have to provide a much more flexible offer – customers want to eat anything or nothing at any time... a restaurateur has to give his customer time, space and choice."

Time. Space. Choice. Let's look at what that might mean for the future of restaurants.

"I REALISED FOOD WAS A MATTER OF A CIVILISED ACHIEVEMENT. THE FRUIT OF CIVILISATION."

MYRTLE ALLEN

THE FUTURE OF RESTAURANTS
time • space • choice

TIME

People eat at all sorts of hours, and they want to eat all sorts of different things during those hours. Whilst it remains broadly true that evening diners want the theatre, the romance and the sociability of a restaurant, and want to make something special of a visit, this is no longer true of daytime customers. Business diners want something, social diners want something else, and the solo diner wants something else again.

You can hold your hands up in the face of this challenge, and say: "Sorry, we don't do that. We are a smart address. We have a business clientele who discuss business – but don't do business – and we have people looking to enjoy a smart lunch. That's what we do."

Fine. But what if the business guys suddenly pull out a bunch of papers, and start sending text messages. And what if they are still in your restaurant at 3.30pm, arguing about something and sending more text messages. What do you do then? And what if the couple having the smart lunch are joined at 2pm by their daughter who got held up at a meeting and who would now like a main course whilst they are having pudding. What do you say? No?

In the future – the near future – some restaurateurs will say no, but many more will say: Yes. The restaurateurs who say no will not necessarily be wrong, for they will be clinging to a concept whereby the customer does things at a time and in a way that suits the restaurant, and they may well be completely unable to cope with any other idea of how a restaurant should function.

But other restaurateurs will be more flexible. Their concept of time will be the customers' concept of time, a flexible, shifting adaptive time, and they will win the business.

SPACE

Formal restaurant rooms are not unlike domestic dining rooms: they have one function, and they cannot easily be adapted to doing anything else. But we have moved away from having dining rooms in our homes, because we rarely used them, and thus they were an expensive waste of space that no longer suited the way we want to live.

Formal restaurant rooms suffer from the same problems. They are only used at restricted times, and they serve only one function: people come in, sit down, are served food, and leave. Until the next service, the room is empty.

Does this sort of arrangement suit the way we eat today? If I want a cup of coffee and a bagel at 10am, why should my choice be confined to coffee shops. And does such an arrangement suit restaurants, organisations which must endeavour to earn decent margins in order simply to survive? If the periods when a restaurant can actually earn money are restricted to, let us say, 11 services per week, their money-making potential is severely limited. They are making life very difficult for themselves.

But what if this restaurant space was multi-functional, offering food for much longer periods of time, right from breakfast or morning coffee straight through lunch, then into an afternoon offer, then early-evening, then dinner.

All of a sudden, you have six potential audiences each day. Not

Ross Lewis, Chapter One Restaurant, Dublin

• Hard work and commitment: these are the foundations of consistency and consistency is the key to long-term success; I stress long term!

• Commitment means living the life of a restaurateur; part-time restaurateurs are generally not successful, at least not in the long term.

• However, living the life brings its own pitfalls: drinking to relieve stress and long working hours being an obvious example. Providing time for outside interests is very difficult, but you must achieve some balance in your life.

• Interpreting your customers' needs and not your own.

• Balance in your food.

• Atmosphere, which depends on interior design, is hugely underestimated yet essential to success. Show me a successful restaurant that has little atmosphere.

• Style of service: the more features your restaurant provides, the more interesting it is for the customer e.g large menu, specialist menus, tasting menus, vegetarian options, oyster counters, reception/bar areas and large amounts of wines by the glass.

• Staff are your greatest resource.

• Communication: meaningful and constant lines of communication (restaurateurs are generally not too good at this).

• Appraisal: essential for progress.

• Training: a programme for training of service and product knowledge at regular and defined intervals.

• Use of suppliers to train staff on their products e.g cheese, coffee, wine.

• Stimulation: make staff feel professional and that they are an important part of the operation. Involve front of house staff in restaurant room work if possible: cutting cheese at the table, making Irish Coffees, etc

• Retention: reliant on all of the above. Other treats include staff outings for meals or visits to artisan producers etc.

• Starting your business the right way: Knowledge of employment law, health and safety legislation, hygiene legislation. An induction manual given to and signed by all new employees helps relay effectively all information, such as above, combined with information specific to your restaurant, e.g uniform, holiday entitlements, disciplinary procedures.

• Accounting systems and advice: Knowing and achieving your margins, estimating your start-up costs accurately (externalities are out of your control – insurance costs, labour costs, interest rates, water/rubbish rates, credit card charges, repairs and renewals. Proper monthly profit and loss accounts; serious discipline needs to be applied to this.

• Marketing / PR: Usual methods for in-house e.g database, special nights. Outside agencies: make sure you get value for money and not simply PR guff with no follow up. You will pay over the top and waste money. A good database is of great use in in-house promotion and helps to develop a relationship with your customers. Marketing is strategically presenting your product to a section of the market you hope to attract.

PR is something you and your staff do every day, either effectively or ineffectively!

• Purchasing: Buy quality goods only, it pays in the long run. Establish a relationship with your suppliers – it also helps in the long run. Take advantage of bulk buying for discount, e.g house wines.

• Personal commitment: The restaurant environment has heavy exposure to stress and there are health implications to be considered.
Your responsibilities as an employer are now greater than ever. You must achieve a balance between work and health. This takes serious discipline, which is probably the most important word in catering.

"I JUST THOUGHT: THIS IS WHAT'S HERE, WHAT WILL WE DO WITH IT? SO I JUST SAY TO THE GROWERS: 'GIVE ME WHATEVER YOU HAVE', AND THEN WE LOOK UP THE BOOKS AND DECIDE WHAT TO DO WITH IT."

CARMEL SOMERS

only that, but if people can pick up food to take away, you also gain further audiences; those who want to take something back to the office at lunchtime, and those who want to bring dinner home in the evening. Now we have eight audiences per day. The space has been maximised.

Some smart people have learnt this lesson already; they have realised that a space can be radically recontextualised. The gastropub boom of the last decade has been built on the simple premise that the premises – the pub – should appeal to more people than just those who wanted to drink. Even before The Eagle in London opened in 1991 and blazed a trail for the modern gastropub that has proved unstoppable, Ann and Franco Taruschio in Abergavenny's legendary Walnut Tree showed that a pub space could be more attractive and more efficient if it could also function as a restaurant. They abolished the distinction between drinking and dining, the belief that the two could not be mutually acceptable. This sort of radical thinking about space – what a space is for, who uses it, when they use it, why they use it – is what is needed by restaurateurs to ensure future restaurants evolve in ways that suit their audience.

CHOICE

Eight audiences a day means people demanding a much broader range of choices, from a single cup of coffee to a party of 20 celebrating an anniversary who want to start with the champagne and take it from there. Is this beyond the range of a standard restaurant kitchen? I don't believe it is.

Restaurants who wish to concentrate on what has become known as "fine dining" won't go down this road, but it is certainly open to many more restaurants to follow the examples of those pioneering restaurateurs who have decided that there is no conflict between creative cooking and serving large numbers of customers.

If you need just one example to prove the theory, the team at Avoca Handweavers manages to cook creatively whilst serving audaciously large numbers of people. In Avoca you can have a coffee and a biscuit, or a three-course lunch with wine. Dublin's AYA sushi bars prove the same point. So does Fishy Fishy Café, so does O'Connell's in Dublin, or Cayenne in Belfast. Offering greater choice does not entail offering lesser quality, and to believe that it does is not merely folly, it is an act of snobbery.

That snobbery accepts that the person who chooses to spend a lot of money on food in a formal setting is entitled to a real culinary experience, whilst the person who wants something quick and inexpensive must be satisfied with the ersatz, with "fast food". Why should that be? The best tapas bars in Spain may serve more conventional cooking than the cutting-edge chefs, but they do what they do with a comparable passion and desire to be the best.

As we shall see later, every restaurant should aim to offer an oasis of pleasure to its customers, irrespective of what they spend or what they want, or when they want it. Some restaurants continue to believe that they are better places if they offer and confer status along with food. They aren't better. They're just more pretentious.

primer

• The rules that have guided the way in which restaurants are run for centuries are changing, and restaurateurs have no option other than to change with them.

• A successful restaurant has many functions, and doesn't confine itself to a dozen services of lunch and dinner per week.

• Think about how your restaurant offers time, space and choice to the customer. Are you making the most of your room and your kitchen?

• A good restaurant can produce creative, imaginative food for many customers: volume doesn't have to compromise cooking into catering.

• Successful restaurants evolve and adapt to changing demands of customers and the pressures of the marketplace: they don't sit still.

2

2

"Cookery is as old as the world,
but it must also remain, always,
as modern as fashion."

PHILÉAS GILBERT

WHAT KIND OF JOB IS IT ANYWAY?

Running a restaurant is one of the most difficult tasks anyone can set themselves. Compared to the multiplicity of disciplines every restaurateur must master, any other job is child's play.

Indeed, I think the fascination we have with restaurants – the fascination we have always had with restaurants – arises precisely because the restaurant-going public acknowledge just how difficult a profession it is.

To make a comparison: a theatre director doesn't have direct charge of the lighting, and he almost never inaugurates the script. He or she will call in a composer to make the music, and a choreographer to make the dance pieces. Someone else will do the costumes. The job of the director is to pull these elements into a unity.

But, in many restaurants, it is common for the restaurateur to be responsible for the design of the room, the script – in this case, the menu and wine offer – the uniforms, the décor, the music, and, for our choreography to work properly, the restaurateur has to train his waiters and waitresses not to bump into one another. And the restaurateur will be in charge of the entire operation, the entire production, day after day, night after night.

No other endeavour demands so much. No other endeavour demands that having a renaissance range of skills is not just what you need to get to the top, but demands that you must have a renaissance range of skills just to get the doors open.

If the rewards were vast, then one could understand why people are attracted to the business of running a restaurant. If restaurateurs pulled down the sort of money that leading lawyers and bankers take for granted, then you could see the point of embarking on a job which takes over your entire life, for that is precisely what running a restaurant does.

But, as anyone in the business knows, the reward for working creatively with natural foods is simply not comparable to that of lawyers or bankers: it is comparable only to the least well-paid jobs in our societies.

So, it takes countless levels of skill, it takes over your life, and it pays badly. Can there ever have been such an unappetising proposition as the business of running a restaurant? Why would anyone, save for the seriously deluded, ever do it?

The answer, of course, is that people do it because, once exposed to the glory of the business, they become, quite simply, addicted to it. Cooking and running a restaurant is not just a job: it is a way of being, and it is a method of artistic expression. Cooks cook just as surely as painters must paint, or musicians must compose or writers must write.

The only obstacle to recognising this fact has been the traditional view that cooking is the practice of a "craft" rather than an artistic endeavour. That is to say: anyone with enough training can do it, and it somehow does not require an inherent gift.

I don't understand this distinction, just as I don't understand that a piece of sculpture can be designated "culture", but a dish of roast suckling pig with a poitin jus, sourced with skill, artistry and care, cooked with skill, artistry and care, and served with skill, artistry and care, is simply "food".

For those who understand what cooking and running a restaurant is all about, the desire to be the instigator of an exciting restaurant is the answer to a creative urge, an artistic need. It is a business that answers the primal need for expression and appreciation.

In his fine book *A History of Cooks and Cooking*, Michael Symons asks why cooks have suffered such neglect from serious analysis and criticism throughout the centuries.

"There are so many texts for, and so few about, cooks. No writer has got up from a meal, so to speak, publicly in awe... Why the neglect?", he asks.

I think that we can answer Mr Symons' question with a brief, contemporary, story, which also illustrates the ways in which our attitudes to cooks and restaurateurs have changed and are changing, and how cooks and restaurateurs are winning the respect and attention – the awe – they deserve. The story also encapsulates the artistic curve of a cooking and restaurant experience.

In late March 2003, as part of a weekend organised by the Slow Food movement in Ireland, a busload of Slow Food members went to eat lunch on Saturday afternoon at Otto's Creative Catering, the coastal restaurant with rooms run by Otto Kunze and his wife, Hilda, near to Butlerstown, in West Cork.

Mr Kunze has lived and worked in Ireland for more than two decades, creating a unique cuisine based on organic and holistic principles. He collects the wild foods that grow around his West Cork restaurant, grows vegetables and herbs and fruits in his polytunnels and vegetable beds, he rears his own rare-breed pigs, chickens cluck all around the yard, and his other foods are all locally produced and sourced.

WHAT KIND OF JOB IS IT ANYWAY?
addiction • artistry • acclaim

Here is the menu for that Saturday lunch:

vegetarian salad platter with organic leaves and various dips,

with chorizo and pepper salami made by Fingal Ferguson,

dry-cured ham made by Frank Krawczyk using our own organic pork,

and Anthony Creswell's Ummera smoked wild salmon

nettle soup

seafood casserole with a Courtmacsherry mixed bag of prawns, monkfish and cod,

flavoured with wild fennel, cream and white wine

cured, smoked and roasted loin of our own pork with apple sauce

lasagne of sea spinach and St Tola organic goat's cheese

vegetables, potatoes and rice

home-made ice creams, and rhubarb crumble with custard and cream

As the lunch came to a conclusion, Mr Kunze was invited to say a few words about his culinary philosophy. Before he could begin, however, the 50 or so people in the room all stood up, quick as lightning, and gave a sustained ovation. A standing ovation. Which lasted for several minutes.

WHAT KIND OF JOB IS IT ANYWAY?
addiction • artistry • acclaim

So, despite what Michael Symons says, anyone who was at Otto's Creative Catering that sunny March afternoon saw people get up "from a meal... publicly in awe".

The ovation for the performance we had just enjoyed shows precisely the artistic curve that is a truly great restaurant experience.

There is, from the artist-cook, the years of study and application – Mr Kunze first learnt his business after riding his bicycle into Kinsale to ask Gerry Galvin, one of Ireland's most creative and influential chefs, for a job in Galvin's restaurant, The Vintage. He started the same way many great restaurateurs do: washing pots.

From this study and learning comes the artistic signature, the unique accents and emphases that make great cooks different one from the other, the individual practice of the skills which means that one can rewrite the culinary rules in your own image.

And then there is the discipline needed to ensure that the performance on the day is perfect, the level of mental acuity needed to ensure that, at the right time, you are on top of your game. This demands, above all else, a perfect control of time and timing, and the ability to orchestrate and choreograph your team, your ingredients, your service.

But, whilst that may make the work sound reminiscent of a dramatic or musical performance, the difference with a restaurant is that everything is done by improvising in time: the script in a restaurant is fluid in terms of timing, and you have to read the changes in the room, the changes in the customers, second by second. The agenda is never fixed, the framework is mobile, the perspective is always altering.

Mercy Fenton, Jacob's on the Mall, Cork

Having been asked, as a restaurateur, my view of the ten things you need to know to run a restaurant successfully, I wonder if I am actually qualified enough to give my opinion.

I am, first and foremost, a chef: that is someone privileged to enforce my taste in food on other people. More recently, I have had experience of dealing directly with the general public.

How do you run a restaurant successfully? It's like the cogs in a watch. All departments must work together, connecting smoothly, each cog knowing its job and understanding the others.

FOOD

As a head chef one must teach and train one's staff, share the knowledge and love of food and take pride in every dish that leaves the kitchen. Promote simple things which are often taken for granted: fresh quality produce, handled with care, sourced well and simply cooked.

Taste, taste, taste! It is impossible to get people to taste food enough and then have them think about it. Does it taste good? Does it taste of what it is supposed to taste of? A silly question, you might think. Not at all. Cooking good food is a conscious effort. Work with your suppliers. Build a relationship that works both for them and for you. Remember that organic potatoes come in all shapes and sizes and those free-range chickens take time to grow. It is real food after all, not something that comes off a production line. Understand seasons and fluctuations and be reasonable. The specialist supplier is our most valued asset.

TEAM

One question I always ask chefs in the kitchen - and myself - when preparing a dish is, would they be happy for their best friend, parents or family to be paying for it? Remember, there are real people beyond the kitchen doors, paying for their meal, whether celebrating, entertaining or on a first date. We must remember our responsibility to the customer, both in the kitchen and in the dining room.

Remember that hard work, long hours (unfortunately) and serious organisation are what keep a good shop going.

Appreciate your staff. Make sure they have a good working environment and a good laugh when the heat is off. Happy chefs cook happy food and happy waiting staff make customers relaxed so everyone wins.

WHAT KIND OF JOB IS IT ANYWAY?
addiction • artistry • acclaim

Be an optimistic leader. Nobody wants to follow a misery-guts.

Be dynamic if you can: bring everything you've got to the party and share it.

Don't be afraid to change track if need be, and don't be afraid to admit it if you're wrong.

CUSTOMERS

Remember, they've come to be entertained and to have a good time. A genuine welcome is an essential first step towards fulfilling that ideal. Most people come in a good mood and if we don't mess it up, they'll leave happy. So preparation and foresight are the keys to success.

Obviously, all the little things add up to the experience, but it should be taken for granted that the simple things are in place: ambience, heating, cleanliness, before you ever accept customers in your door.

You must believe in your product and enjoy delivering it as brilliantly as you possibly can.

Accept that you cannot please all of the people all of the time, but if you can honestly say you did everything possible to meet and surpass their expectations, you will generally have done so.

Then, if all goes well, there is the Holy Grail: has the work managed to persuade the customers to get up "from a meal... publicly in awe"? In Mr Kunze's case, the answer to that was yes, unreservedly so, and what could be sweeter to the soul of a performer than a heartfelt standing ovation.

Thus, the artistic performance was complete, the curve of creativity had commenced, had been executed, and had ended in the most successful and appreciated way.

And for those there on the day, the final element of great art was already in place: an unforgettable memory mixed from sensuality, satisfaction, and respect.

primer

• Cooking is an art, and not simply a craft, so unleash the artistic impulse in yourself and your crew.

• Setting yourself the ambition of achieving a standing ovation for your work is a healthy way to begin.

• You can't be a great cook or restaurateur without serving your time and paying your dues.

• Remember that restaurants are places where you are always improvising in real time: you cannot run a restaurant mechanically.

• Great cooks and restaurateurs are made, not bom.

• Running a restaurant is a performance, with the restaurateur acting as director, script writer and star.

3

3

"Only some restaurants
share the animating spirit,
the restaurantness of a restaurant."

EDWARD BEHR

CREATING A DESTINATION

Some restaurants succeed, many more fail to succeed. Occasionally, the reasons why some places fail are seemingly straightforward: the location is too remote; the food is too experimental; the design of the room is too zany.

But here is the curious thing: there are successful restaurants in every country in the world where remoteness, culinary experimentalism and zany design has people beating down the doors to get in.

Take three Irish examples: did it matter that Bernadette O'Shea's Sligo town restaurant, Truffles, only cooked wildly experimental pizzas during the 1990's?

Does it matter that to actually get to John Desmond and Ellmary Fenton's Island Cottage restaurant in West Cork you have to take a boat and then walk for a mile, only then to be confronted by a no-choice menu eaten in a single tiny room?

Does it hamper Neven Maguire's MacNean Bistro that it is in a remote part of County Cavan, in a village so tiny that you will miss it if you blink whilst driving through?

The answer is: none of these great addresses suffers because of remoteness, experimentalism or zanyness.

So, what they prove is that the rules which people will hand you down for success – location, population base, a broad offer to appeal to a wide cross-section of the public – can all be turned on their head and, in fact, are turned on their head by smart restaurateurs.

So, anyone can open up anywhere and cook anything and be a success, is that right?

No, it isn't. To be a success means creating a destination, a place people want to go to, a room people want to be in, with food that people want to eat and are happy to pay for. If you can get those things right, then it doesn't matter very much where you are, or how unusual your offer is.

So, how do you do it? The answer is that you must have a vision, you must be able to see this perfect destination in your mind's eye, and know how you are going to create it and then run it. Lots of people will deride your vision, especially folk from whom you want to borrow money: don't listen to them.

The destination in all its glory, in all its bold imagining, has to run through your head like a movie.

That great Irish restaurateur, Oliver Peyton has written that in his UK restaurants, which include many of the most high-profile addresses in London, "we cater to a mind set rather than a group based on age, culture or class".

That is a hugely significant statement. Peyton, in other words, isn't just selling you food and drinks – though he sells a very great deal of both – he is actually selling you an idea, a concept that embraces all manner of amorphous things, such as sophistication, romance, style, well-being, hipness, leisure. The food and the drinks come with all these life-style ideas attached to them.

And whose vision of hipness, well-being, style, romance and sophistication are Peyton's tens of thousands of customers buying into? His vision, of course. The vision of a smart guy from County Mayo who knows what the urban sophisticate wants.

A destination, therefore, is not just a physical address. It is an intellectual idea that people want a piece of, regardless of their age, culture or class. Simply creating a good restaurant with decent service, good food and good value will not guarantee you success.

To be a destination, to be a place where people want to be, you have to go further, you have to sell them something that they feel they want, that they feel they need.

All the great destinations do this.

Island Cottage, in addition to outstanding food, sells an adventure that is partly elemental – out on the boat, walking the boreen on Heir Island – and partly theatrical: the curious situation of 22 people, who are for the most part strangers, all eating the same thing in a tiny, age-old cottage on a remote island.

It reads like a movie script, and that is just what every destination address has to do: it has to seem like something scripted as an artistic act.

For Bernadette O'Shea's Truffles restaurant, the script featured world-class culinary brilliance in the most unlikely place, working with the most unlikely ingredients. The best pizzas in the world made in a little room on the north-west coast of Ireland? Let's green light that one.

For Neven Maguire in little Blacklion village, the script includes: the prodigy (he began as a kid); the person finding their element (Mr Maguire was an undistinguished student who becomes the Mozart of the kitchen); the triumph over adversity (the restaurant suffered because of sectarian strife).

So, to be a destination, you have to have a script worthy of a good movie. You have to have an idea, an allure, an attraction that attaches itself to the food and the wine, and which makes people say to themselves: I want that.

primer

• Destination addresses can be created anywhere, so long as you have a vision of exactly what it is that you want to create.

• If, in your mind's eye, you can't see the restaurant packed with punters and pumping with energy on a Friday night, you won't convince anyone that your project is viable.

• A destination address is two things: a reality for the person creating it, and a dream for the person seeking it.

• Don't consider your customers according to their age, culture or class: instead, consider their mind set.

• Along with food and wine, destination addresses also sell well-being, style, romance, sophistication and hipness.

• Destination addresses make people say to themselves: I want that.

4

4

"New-old food in a new-new setting."

JOE BAUM

FOOD & COOKING

There is too much fashion-following in restaurant cookery. Too few cooks, it seems, are determined to be original in their cooking.

Instead, at the time of writing, a whole lot of people in white chefs' jackets want to make foam sauces like Ferran Adria, or they want to do modern Italian food like Giorgio Locatelli, or they reckon a noodle bar would be just whizzo, you know: fast in, fast out, count the profits, never mind the authenticity, all you need is a copy of that book on Asian cooking by that guy from Nahm, David Thompson.

Great cooking doesn't come out of fashion; it comes out of culture: the culture of cuisine and the culture of farming. Of course you must have influences, but those influences must be assimilated, all the better to create a style of cooking that is your own, a style that has your signature.

And the bedrock on which your style is founded must be the very best foods that you have around and about you, wherever you are.

That great Irish chef, Shaun Hill, explains his decision to open his restaurant, The Merchant House, in Ludlow, Shropshire, because, "It was sympathetic to a chef's needs, with a thriving market of good food and people who come to buy it. Good things grow round here. There are game and fish to be had, and first-rate lines of supply for those times of the year when there is little locally. Just as important, there is an interest in food as an ingredient rather than just produce."

Of course, city cooks will say that such an approach is impossible: there simply isn't any food around them, and they must settle for the best that they can get delivered to them from a wholesaler.

Whilst there is an element of truth in this, that element is becoming smaller and smaller as farmers' markets proliferate, and as chefs can begin to create relationships with artisan producers who will grow produce to order for them. For a city cook to assert that you cannot have any specialised produce on the menu is to simply funk out: if you make the effort, you will find the produce and the producers, and if you find it, then it becomes one more element in creating your signature style.

Shaun Hill's remark that "there is an interest in food as an ingredient rather than just produce" is a significant one, but its real significance lies in respect of the way chefs think, rather than the way in which customers think.

For too many chefs, the slippery road to inauthentic, fashionable cooking lies with being unable to distinguish between "ingredients" and "produce". A dry-aged fillet of Angus beef from Pat Whelan's farm in County Tipperary is an ingredient: vac-packed beef of an uncertain provenance is produce. The former will give your cooking a signature; the latter will give you a lot of trouble. We shall see below how using ingredients – distinct, regional, artisan ingredients – help to create a signature menu.

Along with the failure to distinguish between ingredients and produce, the major obstacle to signature cooking is the obsession with newness, with being fashionable. The popular media declare that such-and-such a style of food is now in vogue – tapas; fusion; Balti; Korean – and before you can move every menu has a starter offering stir-fried tortilla with kimchee in a curry sauce.

This sort of nonsense is a particular ailment of our fashion-conscious age. Back in 1996, when so-called "retro-cuisine" was fashionable in the UK, that splendid food writer, Emily Green, wrote "...it should be admitted that retro-cuisine is here, if not exactly new. In more civilised countries, it is known as tradition. Imagine, if you will, Chinese re-discovering the egg noodle, or the people of Marseille opening their morning newspaper to read: 'Bouillabaisse is back'. Would the rich industrialists of Turin ever need to be told, 'Risotto has returned'?"

Ms Green's quote suggests the way in which this point can be taken even further. You eat bouillabaisse in Marseille; you do not eat it in Normandy. Turin is risotto country; Palermo is not.

In other words, the adaptation of a fashionable style of cooking is doubly inauthentic. There is no such thing as "Italian cooking" or "Indian cooking"; there is only the myriad regional styles of cooking found in these countries, based on what local ingredients are the "specialités de la region".

What hope is there for the chef in Belfast or Limerick, then, with his wok and his pasta machine, if he doesn't appreciate this, and is determined to copy the latest trend to be splashed across the weekend glossy magazines? None whatsoever.

This chapter opens with a quotation from Joe Baum, one of the most imaginative and original New York restaurateurs of the last century, for a simple reason: it is the "new-new setting" that should be the fashionable bit of your restaurant, whilst the "new-old food" should acknowledge culinary tradition while simultaneously demonstrating your contemporary take on it: this is where the signature style should be.

Let me try to explain signature style this way. I had the great good fortune, when starting to write this book, to eat a dish of salmon baked in pastry with ginger, cooked by Stephen Markwick. This celebrated fish dish was the invention of George Perry-Smith, one of the most exalted English restaurateurs, and creator of the legendary Hole in the Wall restaurant, in Bath.

The recipe is curious. Two fillets of salmon are placed around a sandwich of currants and chopped-up ginger in syrup, wrapped in pastry and baked, then served with a rich egg yolk and cream herb sauce. The ginger and salmon is an unusual pairing but, having been told that a medieval recipe was the source, Jane Grigson traced the use of ginger with fish back to John Nott's *Cook's and Confectioner's Dictionary* of 1726. (see *Jane Grigson's Fish Book*, 1993, p.314).

Perry-Smith was thus digging deep into culinary history to spring forth the idea for the dish. It became his greatest signature dish, and, according to Jane Grigson, "his other pupils and assistants, with restaurants of their own in various parts of the country, all make this dish with the best local salmon they can buy, as a badge almost of their training." And one of those pupils was Stephen Markwick, who made his version of Perry-Smith's signature dish a particular feature of the menus in his restaurant, Markwick's of Bristol. Mr Markwick revised the sauce, making it without flour as the original recipe dictated, and that was his signature on the signature dish. I ate the dish in Good Things Café in West Cork, where Mr Markwick was cooking for a summer season. It was one of the finest things I have ever eaten.

So, from 1726 via Bath and Bristol and onto West Cork, culinary signatures march onwards.

We could sum it up like this:

Teacher + Pupil + Tradition = Signature.

Paul Flynn, The Tannery Restaurant, Dungarvan, County Waterford

• Do not open a restaurant thinking it is going to make you a millionaire.

• Be aware that it does involve very long, very unsociable hours.

• If you are not a people person, hire someone that is.

• Keeping your labour costs down will be your biggest battle.

• Cook for your customers and not yourself.

• The customer must always leave the restaurant satisfied. Obviously this doesn't always mean just the food. If your customer complains (reasonably), do whatever you have to do to placate them, change the food, don't argue, knock money off, don't charge. You will get the business back off them again if you can turn them around. However, if the customer is a pompous, belligerent, foul mouthed, rude buffoon for whom nothing will please them, suggest they do not come within a mile of your restaurant in the future or your mentally unstable knife wielding kitchen porter will do a job on them.

• Try to maintain a fresh attitude to your premises, dishes and operation. A fresh coat of paint every now and then, changes to the menu, wine list and staff appearance, otherwise your customers will tire of you and move on.

• Try as best you can to maintain consistency with your staff. Treat them well. The same staff make your customers feel comfortable and help to build a bond between the restaurant and customers.

• Pay your suppliers on time and in full. This may sound obvious but you would be surprised at the amount of people in the restaurant business who don't consider this a priority.

• Don't fool yourself. A successful restaurant is a busy restaurant no matter what market it is aiming for.

WRITING A MENU

A good menu should read like a road map. It should not read like a delivery docket.

Sadly, delivery docket menus are everywhere, creating an echo of fast food restaurants inasmuch as they are supplier-oriented, rather than kitchen-oriented.

They offer the chef a painless process to creating a menu: prepared duck breasts; prepared chicken breasts, prepared beef fillets and sirloins; prepared, peeled vegetables, right the way down to prepared sauces and, of course, desserts which the kitchen need have no hand, act or part in preparing. Hotel kitchens love 'em: warm 'em up and ship 'em out, and control that bottom line.

The road map menu, on the other hand, allows for no shortcuts. In fact, it demands a solid store of local knowledge: ducks from that farmer's wife; farmhouse cheese from that producer of raw milk semi-soft cheeses; vegetables from that organic grower's polytunnel; smoked bacon from that smokehouse; local meats from a butcher who will hang the meat to your specification; game from a hunter in season; salad leaves collected that morning.

The road map menu then extends out, hunting down the best chocolate, the best coffee and teas, the best drinks, the best olive oils, anchovies, tuna, dried pulses.

At its very best, a road map menu gives the customer two things. Firstly, it gives a taste of the immediate region, the place where the restaurant is working, and what it can offer to both the cook and the customer.

Secondly, it gives a sense of culinary place. Don't underestimate this. The French, for instance, have based an entire culinary culture on this concept: they call it, specialité de la region. Every great culinary culture comes back, in the end of the day, to its own doorstep. It is, perhaps, the most vital USP of them all, and you can get it for free. It just takes a bit of legwork.

FOOD & COOKING
teacher • pupil • tradition

Here is the sort of thing I mean. This menu is taken from Good Things Café, in Durrus, West Cork:

West Cork Fish Soup

Fingal and Frank's salami

Durrus Cheese, Spinach & Nutmeg Pizza

West Cork Ploughman's

Hederman's smoked salmon with good things

Fish cakes with organic leaves

Good Things salad

Squid with garlic, lemon and parsley

Scones with G's jam and Glenilen clotted cream

Poached cherries with Tipperary organic ice creams

Let's analyse the menu a little to see the depth of culinary and geographical content being offered here.

The West Cork fish soup, for instance, is served with grated Desmond cheese, a super-hard thermophilic cheese made from raw milk in Schull, a few miles from the Café.

Frank and Fingal are, respectively, a salami maker and a bacon and cheese smoker, both of them also working and producing in Schull.

Hederman's smoked salmon is either wild or organic salmon smoked by Frank Hederman in Cobh, East Cork.

The West Cork Ploughman's uses a trio of West Cork cheeses: Milleens from the Beara peninsula, made by Veronica and Norman Steele, the originators of the farmhouse cheese movement in Ireland. From the Sheep's Head peninsula comes Durrus, a raw milk semi-soft cheese made by Jeffa Gill up the hill of Coomkeen. The third cheese is the washed-rind Gubbeen, made by Giana Ferguson in Schull.

Durrus reappears again in the pizza, with organic spinach from a West Cork grower, whilst the Good Things salad features leaves from local organic growers.

Meats and chickens for the Café are delivered from his shop in Bandon by an exemplary butcher, Martin Carey. Fish comes from even closer, either from locals with boats or from the fine Central Fish Market in Bantry.

The scones baked in the Café are served with clotted cream made by Alan and Valerie Kingston on their farm just outside Drimoleague, and they are matched with jams made by Helen Gee of Abbeyleix, County Laois.

Desserts are usually served with scoops of Tipperary Organic Ice Cream, made near Thurles, County Tipperary by Paddy and Joyce O'Keeffe.

Amongst the drinks on offer are the rare apple juices and a very dry cider made by Con Traas of The Apple Farm, in County Tipperary. There are beers and the fabulous O'Hara's stout from the Carlow Brewing Company, and milk from a local farmer. The teas are the peerless blends of Barry's of Cork, a long-established and very successful family firm of tea blenders.

FOOD & COOKING
teacher • pupil • tradition

The food, then, is a road map of the immediate zone around the Café - West Cork cheeses, salad leaves, meats, salamis and fish - abetted by icon-standard artisan products from farther afield. Even before you eat the food, you know exactly where you are, and you also know the sort of culinary standards exacted by owner Carmel Somers.

Here, by way of contrast, is what some people reckon passes for a menu:

Cream soup of the day

Golden fried brie with a Cumberland sauce

Creamy Atlantic seafood chowder

Caesar salad

Julienne of smoked chicken with cashew nuts on a bed of tossed seasonal salad

10oz fillet steak

smoked chicken and mushroom tagliatelle

pan roasted barbary duck breast garnished with a honey ginger glaze

baked medallions of monkfish with beurre blanc

tenderloin of lamb with a redcurrant sauce

all above served with vegetables and potatoes

dessert platter

Appetising, is it not? That's right: it's not appetising in the slightest. This isn't a menu: it's a train crash of anonymous ingredients colliding with half-baked culinary skills in a stew of inappropriate language.

Astonishingly, in our sophisticated world, this sort of menu remains common. Anonymous, anodyne and bland, it is as uninformative as any document containing written language can possibly be.

What exactly is in that soup? Where does the lamb come from, or the steak? Reckon they made a Caesar dressing from scratch according to Caesar Cardini's edict? Or do you think they gave the jar a shake and poured it over some God-forsaken leaves? Reading this sort of thing makes you want to curl up on that bed of tossed seasonal salad leaves, and die.

The only person happy to see a menu like this is the supplier of the barbary duck breast and the Caesar dressing and the dessert platter and all the rest of the stuff that can be ticked off on the delivery docket.

"PRODUCE IS THE BACKBONE OF MY COOKING AND AROUND HERE I HAVE THE BEST PRODUCE. I LIKE TO SHOW THE INGREDIENTS OFF."

NEVEN MAGUIRE

FOOD & COOKING
teacher • pupil • tradition

"To me, menus are a language unto themselves," writes Jeremiah Tower. "Reading an old menu slowly forms in my mind's eye its era, the sensibility of the restaurateur or chef, even the physical details of the dining room."

To be able to provoke such a reaction should be the aim of every menu. Just take a look at this menu, for example, from Andoni Luis Aduriz's extraordinary Mugaritz restaurant, close to San Sebastian in the Basque country. Look at how it reveals its era, the profound culinary sensibility of Aduriz, even the physical nature of this sublime restaurant:

Platter of "Joselito" premium Spanish cured ham. Rva. 1998

Vegetables, oven roasted and raw, sprouts and leaves, wild and cultivated, seasoned with hazelnut butter and dusted with seeds and petals. Emmenthal cheese generous season

Squid and bread fisherman's gel. Sautéed squid; orchard's shoots and simple grains of paradise

Tempered buffalo milk mozzarella and sautéed mushrooms upon a milky leave. Meat juice and *Spilantes acmella* oil

Reproducing an aroma from our environment: Roasted lamb fillet. Shredded sweet garlic, chlorophyll whipped with hazelnut oil; (Oxtalis acetosella) and toasted hazelnuts

Selection of wide variety of Euskalherria cheeses: Small portions of homemade ewe, cow, goat and buffalo milk cheeses, abbey, monastery and farmhouse cheeses, mountain and meadow cheeses

Sun-ripened, season's red fruit with the sharp contrast of white pepper ice-cream. Chillied lilaceous soup

primer

- **Every great restaurant has a signature style of cooking, and signature dishes.**

- **Don't confuse ingredients with produce. Ingredients are distinctive: produce is uniform.**

- **A menu should read like a road map, and not a delivery docket.**

- **Every menu should reveal its time, the sensibilities of the owner or chef, and the spirit of the restaurant.**

- **Fashion-following is the enemy of good, creative cooking. Your room should be fashionable: your cooking should be authentic.**

- **Artisan produce and artisan producers are a restaurateur's greatest ally.**

- **Teacher + Pupil + Tradition = Signature.**

- **Specialité de la Region is the greatest USP of them all.**

5

5

"Unlike many chefs, George treated his staff with great respect. He addressed everyone by name, and made us feel that our contribution was essential to the success of the restaurant."

JOYCE MOLYNEUX ON GEORGE PERRY-SMITH

SERVICE

The relationship between many restaurants and customers is a curious one. In a commercial world where anyone selling a product seeks ways in which to incentivise the relationship with the customer, via special offers, club cards, discounts, you name it, restaurants seem to believe that they don't need to bother to do any of that stuff. They cook your dinner, you pay for it, and leave. Thanks.

Restaurants are wrong, and some smart restaurateurs have realised that if you work on incentivising the relationship, then you have a lot to gain.

I discussed this question with Yoichi Hoashi, proprietor of Dublin's AYA sushi bars and delis. Here is how Yoichi sees it:

RESPECT

"At the end of the day, customers have to be respected", says Mr Hoashi. "But the challenge is: how do you make that tangible?"

How indeed. The thorny problem of how restaurants relate to their customers is one of the most difficult, and seemingly most intangible, in the whole restaurant business. Restaurants need customers, but short of serving them food, they usually don't seem to know how to treat them, and how to deal with them on an on-going basis. Mr Hoashi has the answer.

"In Japan, because there are simply so many people and so many businesses, every company's communication is focused on the customer", says Mr Hoashi. "And regular contact is the basis of that relationship. This is something I simply know from my Japanese background."

This insider information led Mr Hoashi to establish a regular diner scheme, in the late 1980's, at the parent restaurant of AYA, the Ayumi-Ya in Blackrock, in south County Dublin. This simple practice, whereby people who ate regularly at the Ayumi-Ya qualified for free meals, has been revolutionary, but for Hoashi it is his way "of creating that tangible relationship between restaurant and customer".

If the regular diner scheme worked in Blackrock, it has given the impetus to a rash of smart marketing practices in AYA.

For a start, Hoashi created the little figure of AYA, the smiling stick figure with the up-turned wok as a hat. The first time my seven-year-old daughter caught a glimpse of AYA, she sat right down and drew a version of him straight away. Cereals manufacturers and sweetie barons would kill for such an instantaneous and positive reaction from a child.

The figure of AYA isn't just marketing; it's conceptual magnificence. Suddenly, Hoashi wasn't selling people the awkward and distinct and unknown idea of a conveyor belt sushi bar. He was giving them a friend.

AYA was suddenly not a place where you got wet rice and raw fish and seaweed and all that weird stuff which the Irish wouldn't eat in a fit. AYA was a place where you got... well, AYA.

The ideas are all aimed "at offering people little bits of AYA, at whatever level they want and at whatever level they can afford. Students like certain elements. Shoppers like others. There is simple food, and serious food."

There is the hour-by-hour sushi week card, for example, which tells you that between certain hours on certain days you can get two of bottles of Asahi beer for the price of one. It tells you that the week features a cluster of "Happy Zones" when all sushi dishes have a reduced price. Pop in during a Sushi 55 period, and you have 55 minutes of unlimited eating plus a drink.

"It's feasible for customers to get to us at the level they can afford", says Hoashi. "Sushi 55 has really become a club, a place where everyone gets a ticket worth 2 points and when you collect 20 points you get free sushi." Simple, and so obvious.

Restaurateurs, just as confused about punters as Freudians are about women, spend their time asking "What do customers want?" Yoichi Hoashi understands that customers just want to be looked after.

"Nothing of this requires marketing," Hoashi asserts. "It's just understanding your market."

What it proves is that Yoichi Hoashi understands his market. All his efforts are dedicated to "getting to know our customers. AYA has 2,500 customers each week, and we want to know them personally."

So, the office workers and retail assistants who pack out the deli at AYA to get their food-to-go are rewarded with sambo combo offers, with savings on various foods, and they can collect points every time they buy in order to collect a sushi-pack, a ready dinner, a sushi party pack or an AYA T-shirt. "I definitely want to see more AYA T-shirts on the street!" laughs Mr Hoashi.

THE T-SHIRT

What a simple idea: T-shirts bearing the name of your local restaurant. But, with the exception of AYA, restaurants just don't do that sort of thing. They don't go for rewards and special offers, they don't discount in order to bring in off-peak dining. They don't, in short, use any of the sophisticated marketing measures which retailers have had to resort to in order to build market share and keep off the competition. Restaurateurs seem to want to continue to live in an ivory tower, doing what they do, and no more than what they do.

But, can they continue in this way? And, if they do, then what are they missing out on?

The biggest threat that comes from not using marketing techniques is simple and spectacular; your restaurant will not succeed, or it may succeed only until greater competition comes along to threaten your existence. If the guy down the street is offering more than you, and marketing it to his customers in a slick way, then the chances are your days are numbered: he will prosper, you will steadily fail.

Retailers have their heads stuffed with research on the psychology of the shopper and how to make a successful proposition to them. Restaurateurs treat all that stuff as so much mumbo-jumbo.

Restaurateurs have always been, and remain, slow to grasp the importance of marketing. Many seem to believe that the restaurant experience is not comparable to any retail experience, that it is somehow different from the way in which people spend money anywhere else, and thus doesn't have to play by the same rules.

This is not true: restaurants compete with each other for customers, and compete with other retail offers for the people's dollar. And so, you must have your own list of USPs: Unique Selling Points. And, just as importantly, you must get the message across.

SERVICE
respect • reward • retain

One area of endeavour that used to be comparable to running a restaurant was the business of writing books. Author writes book, publisher publishes it, end of story.

But there is no author alive today who doesn't engage in whatever marketing is necessary in order to sell his or her book. Once you have written it, then you get on the road and sell it. Writing novels and books isn't an ivory tower occupation any more: if you don't sell, your contract gets torn up.

Restaurants have to understand that in order to succeed – and to keep succeeding – you have to use whatever marketing will work for you. T-shirts? Discounts? Loyalty cards? Visits by your suppliers to the restaurant to chat to the customers? Free wine? Charity events? Supporting community projects?

In a changing marketplace, you must keep changing, and the best way to keep your customers is to keep engaging your customers. Don't test their loyalty by pushing it too far. If you do, the chances are you will discover they aren't loyal at all.

"TO MAKE PEOPLE HAPPY. THAT'S WHAT COOKING IS ALL ABOUT."

THOMAS KELLER

Turlough McNamara and Jennifer McNally,
Coast Restaurant and Townhouse, Tramore, County Waterford

The question of what ingredients combine to create successful restaurants occupies the thoughts of many would-be restaurateurs to the same extent that the vexed question of what makes a perfect béarnaise concerns would-be chefs and cooks.

For our part, we enjoyed eating in a great many restaurants and many great restaurants before getting stuck in to creating Coast in Tramore. In fact, a mega-review covering some of our gastronomic research could probably occupy a reasonably-sized if not necessarily gripping book in its own right!

Anyhow, this is not that book so to the question at hand – What are the 10 things you need to know to run a restaurant successfully?

In no particular order, some of the items we'd suggest would-be operators look at fairly closely include…

PEOPLE

This is probably the ultimate people business. The dishes we serve are created by people from ingredients supplied to us by people. These dishes are in turn presented to our customers (people in their own right,

of course) by a whole new set of people. Given all of this, the importance of having a good team with the right attitude can not be stressed enough and selection of personnel deserves great attention – particularly in the vital early stages of a restaurant's life. A suggestion is to concentrate on picking a team that will work well together rather than a collection of great individuals who are just that - individuals. While you should be able to equip your team with specific skills over time, there is no training for attitude and passion so a good guide might be to hire for attitude.

FOOD

While the standard of service provided is clearly a significant and reasonably measurable part of the restaurant mix, and an opportunity to set your offering apart from that of competitors, it is unlikely that average or below-par food served superbly will prove a winner in the marketplace. There is a growing recognition that the restaurant trade is not simply about "food, food, food and food again" but there is not a successful restaurant in Ireland or elsewhere that doesn't pay huge attention to their menus. Each dish needs to be right – right not just on the well-honed palate of the chef but right on the palates of diners who may range in age from 18 to 80 and in experience of haute cuisine from a well-travelled executive to a non-passport holder who eats out twice a year. Keep your food offering simple, locally-focused and in season. Following on from this, you will be able to concentrate on presentation and rely on the food growing with your business.

DÉCOR AND DESIGN

People and food combine to make great restaurants; décor can add the vital ingredient that makes sure great restaurants are great businesses with a strong repeat trade. The surroundings you create for customers need to make them feel comfortable and at home in what is inevitably a more formal environment than they will ordinarily eat in.

The phrase "a home away from home" is worn beyond repair and, dare I say it, a touch over-relied on by food and accommodation critics. However, that is what restaurateurs must strive to offer and effective design and décor will be vital ingredients in getting the mix just right.

While the range of television programmes featuring home revamps suggests that we are turning into a nation of would-be interior designers, there is rarely a substitute for professional advice when it comes to getting the "look" and "feel" of a restaurant just right. The winning combination will involve good ideas put

forward by ambitious operators being sketched out and implemented by professional and highly skilled designers and decorators. A key issue here should be matching your décor and design to the intended food offering at your restaurant. Consider what will make sense.

Design and décor are not a constant and it is vital for successful restaurants to carefully monitor current trends and to keep an eye on innovative "looks" being introduced by peer restaurants at home and overseas. If we agreed earlier that "Food, food, food..." was not the perfect mantra for restaurant management then perhaps "Detail, detail, detail..." might make a fitting replacement.

PRICING

"How much is enough to charge?" This question must rank highly among the top 10 most frequently asked when restaurateurs gather! While the answer too often seems to be a flippant "As much as you think you'll get away with", pricing deserves more attention than this and successful restaurateurs invariably keep a close watch on – among other things: market trends, ingredient prices, labour and operating costs when considering how to price various menu offerings.

The bottom line, however, ought to be "What represents value and equity?" The question to pose should perhaps be "What is a reasonable price for this dish that I am offering, taking account of what it has cost to serve and what it is worth to my customer?"

A distinction should be made between value and price. Good value is not inextricably linked to low prices. Indeed, some of the best value eating experiences in Ireland and elsewhere come in mid- to high-end restaurants that are not cheap but provide real value-for-money.

LOCATION

The likelihood is that before you look at getting the right people, the best possible menus, the cutting-edge décor and design and the pricing structure just right, you will want to consider where best to locate your restaurant. Do you break the bank and go for that fantastic Georgian townhouse that you know is coming on the market in a great part of town or do you check out that disused warehouse that could be transformed with the right people at the helm? Then there's the former wine-bar that's near some big office developments and got a lot of early evening trade when it was open.

So many premises, so many choices – but only one of them can be the right one for your operation. Issues to consider when you're checking out possible locations include: What will work in the space?; Who am I looking to attract?; Where do the customers I am chasing live?; What's the transport situation for customers needing to get home after a late meal?; How many customers do I need to serve to make the business pay its way?; Are we going for a strong day- or evening-trade?; What's the weekend/weekday mix going to be? Having looked at some of the business issues underpinning location decisions, you will need to devote considerable attention to what type of building you're going for.

We wrote earlier about the importance attached to design and décor. The range of options open to operators in this regard will be dictated in large part by the building they select as their base. Given this, it would seem wise to involve design specialists alongside architects and surveyors when you are viewing properties. They [designers] can provide insights that are unlikely to be offered by other professionals.

Other considerations of varying importance include the availability of suitable personnel in the neighbourhood; the nature of existing businesses occupying adjacent buildings; the visibility of the property and the likelihood that its use as a restaurant will attract enquiring customers you can convert to regulars.

In any event (and here we're stealing the favoured line of estate agents and then twisting it), ahead of opening a restaurant you may feel it's a case of "Location, location, location". The reality, however, is that it will be equally important to become part of the locality and neighbourhood in which you operate. While visitors and business clients may be the icing on the cake it could well be that it is your geographic neighbours that help to both lay the foundations for your trade and to build additional storeys over time. We're in danger of going in to cheesy overdrive here but perhaps it's a case of "Neighbours... everybody needs good neighbours".

ATMOSPHERE

You've got your building and you're pretty sure you've got the rest of the ingredients just right as well. How though do you create the sort of "home away from home" atmosphere that we mentioned about earlier without going down the supposedly cosy, faux Irish route?

Alongside reputation, the atmosphere of a successful restaurant is generally one of its most valuable intangible assets and deserves a column all of its own in any restaurant's annual returns to the Companies Office and Revenue! While the importance of atmosphere is accepted by all but the most naïve of potential restaurateurs, there are very mixed views on what the "magic ingredients" are which create an atmosphere that wins you the loyalty of a very diverse customer base.

Issues to examine – and again, early on is the time to get it right if you can – include seating layout; spatial management; drinks areas; materials and colours used for soft

furnishings and wall hangings; artwork; food style; signage and branding; music (style, variety and volume); the disposition, knowledge and age profile of front-of-house personnel; the tone and wording of menus and, once again, our stalwarts...décor and design.

MARKETING AND PUBLICITY

The perceived wisdom may be that there's no substitute for word-of-mouth and in rural and urban settings alike this is certainly a very valuable source of business. However, for a restaurant that's just about to open or which has just opened, the question is more likely to be "How do we get the mouths of key influencers open and working for us in the first place?"

Again, there are almost as many approaches as there are restaurants and it may be that you decide to engage the services of a marketing/public relations company at the outset (if so, perhaps you should go for one with event management and previous restaurant/hospitality experience).

However you proceed, some of the actions you may want to look at include relatively low-key advertising of specific events and themed nights; seeking editorial coverage from food critics attached to relevant print media; issuing upbeat media releases locally when you open and if/when national media organisations favour you with a positive review; hosting corporate and media familiarisations; using your front-of-house staff and their families as "local ambassadors" and inviting targeted local community leaders to an open evening when they get to sample and – hopefully – enjoy your offering.

CONTINUOUS IMPROVEMENT

Let's forward gaze…you've set up your restaurant and had a good first six months. The buzz is proving addictive. You're working hard but loving it. How then do you ensure that the light doesn't dim on your business and that you don't become one season wonders who snatched defeat from the jaws of victory?

"Sustaining Excellence" sounds like the title for a business conference that you may or may not want to attend but what it should perhaps be is your credo for maintaining and building on your business success. Attention to detail, sometimes to the point of near-obsession, is vital if your restaurant's honeymoon period is to prove the foundation of a rewarding marriage that holds the attention of you and your spouse (the customers).

Rather than simply striving to hold levels at what they were when you opened or shortly afterwards, why not set a goal of being five per cent better every six months. How you rate this is your own business, but be firm and fair with yourself and your staff – for instance, don't accommodate slipping standards on the basis that it's been a busy period or you are short-staffed.

Rather, set it as your goal that the experience of your restaurant enjoyed by diners will be at the highest possible level whether they come in on a busy Saturday night or a wintry Tuesday when they may have much of your property and attention to themselves.

Do it informally or have a written code but please do it – develop your business continually and ensure that every night's show is better or, at a minimum, as good as the previous night's.

SIMPLICITY

While it comes second from last in this list, simplicity might in fact be an underlying theme. "Keep it simple" is perhaps the single most important piece of advice we would offer to would-be restaurateurs. Don't run before you can walk. Provide the best offering you can from day one but don't try to take on Michelin-starred restaurants that have built up their reputations and trade over decades. Rather, do a small number of things extremely well and gradually you will grow in confidence and your range will expand accordingly.

Unless the fundamentals are right and kept right, you can and will not hope to develop a sustainable business model that will serve you as well in year three and year seven as it did in year one.

Over-elaboration, complicating simple situations and adding unnecessary layers are all recipes for high stress and low prospects of success.

To take an example, if your space will accommodate 50 diners at a squeeze or 30 in comfort, limit your capacity at the lower number.

You will be providing a better night out and, while it's to a smaller number, they will be back. Offering a positive experience to, say, 25 of the 30 must beat offering a sauna-style night out to 50 customers, only 10 of whom may ever return.

DETERMINED ATTITUDE

There are many things needed to create and maintain a successful restaurant and we hope we've touched on at least some of them here.

Most of all though you'll need a good attitude to hard work, a sense of humour and strong nerves for those times when the pressure is on from the kitchen on the one hand and hungry diners on the other!

Human endeavour being what it is there will inevitably be knocks as you travel on what can be a bumpy road strewn with failed attempts to create the ultimate eating experience.

You too will have nights that you know have not seen your restaurant put on the best possible show. However, if you are a natural-born restaurateur you will get up earlier than usual on the following morning, take a look at what could have been done better the previous night and work twice as hard that day to make sure your next night is your best yet.

Restaurateurs compete in a difficult and challenging marketplace.

In some respects, we as a profession are front-line public servants in the semi-formal meaning of the phrase. To meet our responsibilities to our customers requires a positive mental attitude; to keep doing it requires mental toughness and physical strength as well as flexibility and adaptability.

A well-known public relations guru once stated that success in that profession went to those with "balls of iron and a spine of steel".

While his political correctness and gender awareness was questionable on that occasion, the gentleman in question might well have been talking about the restaurant trade!

To the list though should be added "and a winning attitude".

Go for it and good luck !

READING CHARLIE TROTTER

As far as Edmund Lawler, author of *Lessons in service from Charlie Trotter* is concerned, a visit to Charlie Trotter's restaurant in Chicago is better than sex, and they also park your car.

The book suffers from an infection of hagiography rarely seen outside teen pop magazines, combined with a gadgetry fixation more suited to motoring magazines; on page 62, Lawler tells us that Trotter's kitchen is "state-of-the-art". Just in case we haven't got it yet, he then tells us once more, seven lines later.

The book's reverence for Trotter is matched only by the utter humourlessness of the text: time and again, Lawler lets slip the opportunity to deflate the self-importance of all concerned.

I mean, if Charlie tells you that *Apocalypse Now* and *Fitzcarraldo* are his two favourite movies, shouldn't you ask: "What's wrong with *Bringing Up Baby*?".

And if the great man then tells you that Dostoyevsky is the writer who has had the greatest influence on his thinking, shouldn't you suggest he tries to get out more?

But, this is an American book, Charlie Trotter is a hugely successful American cook and businessman, so no fun is poked anywhichway. Instead, Lawler gives us the Trotter line over a couple of hundred pages that are profoundly repetitious.

But, Charlie Trotter's is not a legendary destination address for no reason, and if Lawler is uncritical, Charlie Trotter and his crew are intensely self-critical, which gives the book some balance, and which reveals some service attitudes and practices I think worth dwelling on.

SERVICE
respect • reward • retain

"The cuisine, the wine, the ambience, and the service... No one of those elements do we consider more important than the other."

I would add a fifth element to this – value – a factor which is likely to be less of a consideration in a top-dollar destination like Trotter's. But, the key element here is the necessary balance between all these elements of the entertainment.

This question of balance between the essential elements that make a restaurant work is echoed by several of the testimonies by restaurateurs in this book, and it seems to me to have been the biggest wake-up call to restaurateurs in the last decade.

Previously, for instance, restaurants tolerated prima donnas in the kitchen, men who reckoned that they were more important than everyone else, and who treated everyone with a lack of respect because they believed they were top dog.

But restaurants only work at their best when everyone's effort is respected and valued, and when you have a crew working towards one defined goal. Charlie Trotter may be the top dog in his place, but he doesn't behave like it.

So, if your primary qualification is as a cook, consider all the things that you do not know. What are your weaknesses, and how do you cure them? If you are a kitchen person who dreads front-of-house, then get someone good for f-o-h, and don't ever believe that it can simply look after itself: nothing in a restaurant looks after itself, everything has to be looked after.

"THE WHOLE EVENING IS AN ACCUMULATION OF SMALL DETAILS"

Exactly. So, if your bathrooms aren't up to scratch, you threaten wrecking someone's big night out. Everything counts, and you must focus on all the details, rather than lazily paying attention to the seemingly more important things: every detail is important, the smallest gestures can make someone feel special.

"THE LITTLE THINGS COST... NOTHING."

It costs nothing to hang someone's coat, to order them a cab, to make a wine recommendation if a person looks ill at ease with the wine list, to wrap up some food they haven't eaten so they can bring it home, to be courteous, to check the bathroom. These actions have no cost, but their value is immense in an entertainment such as a restaurant.

"TRICKS OF THE TRADE CAN CONVERT FIRST-TIME VISITORS INTO LOYAL CUSTOMERS."

Creating loyal customers is the aim of every successful restaurant, but you won't do it simply through good cooking. It is service that creates a loyal customer, it is service that makes a guest feel comfortable, welcome and valued, and that brings them back time and again.

The loyal customer spends more and is easier to deal with than the slightly apprehensive newcomer, so don't devote more time to the new guest: make sure the loyal customer has as much, if indeed not more, of your time. Put it this way: the loyal customer is your bread and butter; the newcomer is just the cherry on the icing on the cake.

"CHECK THEIR EGOS AT THE DOOR IF THEY EXPECT TO BE ON TOP OF THEIR GAME."

Or, don't forget that it's all about the customer, and not about you. Sadly, many restaurants are created as vanity exercises by people who imagine it is a glamorous and easy profession. They visualise themselves swanning around the room chatting with celebs.

These people like to use the large amounts of money they have made, in banking, or cement production, or water treatment and the like, to build monuments to themselves. Unfortunately, because they have lots of money, they can frequently keep these restaurants running for considerable periods of time.

Vanity projects are not real restaurants, and they never operate at the top of their game. People in the restaurant business are there to serve the customer, and doing so means checking your ego at the door.

It also means checking your worries at the door: if your dog has just died or your spouse has just run off with her life coach, it is your problem, not the customer's. The show must go on.

"ULTIMATELY, SERVICE IS A HALLMARK OF CIVILISATION."

This quote, from Kurt Sorensen, one of the sage voices captured in the book, chimes perfectly with the quote from Myrtle Allen, of Ballymaloe House, earlier in this book: "I realised food was a matter of a civilised achievement. The fruit of civilisation".

How correct Sorensen is to apply the hallmark of civilisation to the art of service. And service, like cooking, is an art, a noble art.

"I VIEW SERVICE AS GIVING MORE THAN WHAT IS EXPECTED."

This quote from Jason Platt summarises exactly what makes the best service so successful and memorable: it over-delivers. If the customer gets what they expect, and no more, you haven't done enough to create a loyal customer. Over-delivering on service should be the norm in every restaurant.

"A REPRIMAND IS MEANT AS INSTRUCTION."

Every employee has got to understand that they are going to make mistakes, and that whilst mistakes are forgivable, they are not repeatable. Don't reprimand someone just to tell them off; turn it into an analysis of what went wrong and why, and make sure they know how to ensure that it won't happen again. It's part of the pressure they have to learn to take if they want to be on top of their game.

"HE BELIEVES IN THE RISK OF HIRING PEOPLE WITH NON-TRADITIONAL BACKGROUNDS."

If the choice is between the culinary graduate who came top of his class, or the 29-year-old banker who loves food and has come to hate her job, the person who may turn out to be most successful is the banker rather than the class star.

Creative cooking demands something more than the ability to loop through exams. It takes a sense of hunger, and a sense of risk: the 29-year-old is going to give it everything she has got; the class star may feel they have already arrived.

Plus, the banker has the experience of different ways of thinking, whereas the new graduate is simply proficient in one field. But restaurants work best when people are multi-skilled, and when they can work and think in an abstract, analytical way, and when they can change, and keep changing. If people are too deeply into the culture, they may never appreciate the shortfalls of the culture.

"HE HAD A GUT INSTINCT THAT SHE 'GETS IT'."

"Getting it" is one of the key stages of educating and empowering an employee.

I was once doing a wine tasting with a manager and a bunch of extremely raw recruits who were to be the floor staff in a new hotel restaurant, one of whom, John, "didn't like wine". "You have to taste it anyhow," we told him, and began to pour, taste and explain the wines.

By the third glass, John had "got it". It only took three small tastes of different varietals for him to realise that he had never tasted proper, artisan wines before, and the moment the magic hit, we had him: he "got it." I expect to hear any day now that he's going to aim for the M.W.

"IF THE APPLICANT... FAILS TO HELP CLEAR CUPS, GLASSES, OR NAPKINS FROM THE TABLE..."

Then they don't get a job at Charlie Trotter's, and you, likewise, should never employ anyone who reckons such tasks are someone else's work.

The ability to do six things at once, which is the hallmark of a true restaurant person, can be improved, but it really has to be there in an instinctual sense: a real restaurant person never waits for anyone else to do a task, never walks past a table that can be cleared, never fails to look at situations where they can assist. If the interviewee gets up and doesn't help to clear up, don't employ them.

And, of course, when you are interviewing potential staff, always make sure coffee and mineral water and plates of things to eat are in play. The interviewee may do a tickety-boo interview, and then reveal their weakness right at the end.

respect • reward • retain

"IT'S A CONTINUING EDUCATION."

If staff get bored, then you have a problem. You won't be able to motivate them, or get them to do anything other than going through the motions.

So, they have to be exposed to the vocational aspects of the job, they have to see that with food and wine, you can always go deeper, learn more, experience more and, thus, get more out of the job. Staff need to work stages in other restaurants, they need to do whatever extra-curricular study will help them in their career – this is especially true of anyone who wants to work with wine. They need to be exposed to icon practitioners from whom they can learn.

"TROTTER LIKES TO REHIRE TALENTED FORMER EMPLOYEES."

This is the "boomerang factor": love 'em, and let 'em go. If you do, they will not only be back, but when they come back they will have gained broader experience – hopefully in fields other than restaurants – and they will likely also better appreciate what it is you do, and respect it more.

Boomerangers make better workers, whether you are running Charlie Trotter's or welcoming past pupils back as teachers in the Ballymaloe Cookery School or wherever. So, if they get burned-out, or curious or disenchanted, buy them a rucksack and a return ticket.

78   HOW TO RUN A RESTAURANT

"Nothing is below anyone, including Charlie Trotter, whom I've seen clear tables or bring food to tables."

The first time I ever saw Myrtle Allen, of Ballymaloe House, it was about 8.30pm on a Saturday night, and Mrs Allen was clearing a table in the restaurant. The greatest Irish restaurateur of them all was doing what all great restaurateurs do: she was being part of the team.

You will see the same thing in the legendary Kelly's Hotel in Rosslare, where Bill Kelly leads from the front, as his family have done for more than a century. Every truly great restaurant, in other words, abolishes the idea of a hierarchy, and that is what makes them great restaurants.

"They don't have to come and justify their decision... they are empowered to make that call in the moment..."

Staff need to be trusted, otherwise you can't make a restaurant work, and if that means that they have the power to cancel a bill because something went wrong, or to offer complimentary drinks because someone has been kept waiting, then it has to be their call.

If the decision has to ascend a chain of command, it will be robbed of the spontaneity necessary to keep a situation under control, and will be worthless to the customers. And having everything referred to a management figure places too much of a burden on that person.

Again, we have to go back to the idea of a crew working together, but each of whom has the ability to make autonomous decisions. Anyone who watched the great Dutch football team of the early 1980's, with their scintillating brand of "total football" will know exactly what I mean.

"SUCCESSFUL BUSINESSES CULTIVATE A SENSE OF LOYALTY AMONG THEIR CUSTOMERS."

They do this out of naked self-interest – it is easier and cheaper to keep an existing customer than to spend time and effort capturing a new one – and also because it is one of those things that gives a room atmosphere: relaxed people enjoying food and wine in a familiar place will make the room work for you. And what creates loyalty? Service. Personal, individual, respectful, professional service.

"THE 1,500 PEOPLE IN THE DATABASE RECEIVE MAILINGS ABOUT SPECIAL EVENTS AT THE RESTAURANT."

The use of a customer database is dealt with in this book in the media management section, but it is worth dwelling on the point that a restaurant such as Charlie Trotter's, where one has to book weeks in advance to secure a table, still makes those prized 1,500 customers feel special by letting them into new information first off. In fact, Trotter even sends them Christmas cards. Excessive? Well, if you had a regular customer for your goods and services who spent a considerable amount of money with you year after year, you would likely send them an christmas gift. Why should a restaurant customer be viewed in a different way? They shouldn't.

"IT'S IMPORTANT TO GET THE GUEST TO RELAX..."

This is especially true if you run a smart establishment: just remember that many people can be intimidated by grandness, and when they are intimidated they are nervous and when they are nervous they aren't relaxed, and that makes them a zillion times more difficult to deal with.

This is where the proposition element comes into play: take responsibility off them by continually proposing solutions, in order to make them relax.

"YOU'RE HERE TO SERVE THE GREAT CAUSE..."

This applies whether you are a short-order cook in a breakfast bar, the guy who makes the cocktails or the plongeur. The nobility of any cause is actually created by the staff who work in it, and the sort of respect they feel they are worthy of.

If they serve the cause, if they pull together, then they win. Organisation amongst all the elements is the key here, for organisation amongst all the disparate parties is what makes one team a winner, from politics to sport to the greatest game of them all: running a restaurant.

"IF YOU LET A TABLE GET OUT OF CONTROL, IT CAN SPARK A CHAIN REACTION."

For every dozen tables of happy, shiny people determined to have the time of their lives, there will be a table of grumpy, doesn't-matter-what-you-do types who will only get a kick if they can spread their dissatisfaction with themselves, their guest, their life. You cannot let that dissatisfaction spread through the room: when you spot it, you must contain it, for otherwise it can spread like an oil spill. This is the most thankless task in service, but also one of the most important. The chance of winning old misery guts around is small, so this is a containment exercise: you can't make them have fun, but don't let them spoil everyone else's.

"TROTTER HAS TWEAKED THE CALCULUS OF THE DINING ROOM BY 'FIRING' CERTAIN CATEGORIES OF GUESTS."

If there are individuals who disturb your dining room, through various aspects of their behaviour, don't let them through the door, and don't be slow to fire them. Some folk will insistently criticise and belittle your best efforts and then, incredibly, they will be there again next Saturday night. Send them packing.

"OVER-SERVICE IS AS BAD AS UNDER-SERVICE."

Over-delivering on the totality of the experience is what you want to achieve, but if this means getting in your customer's hair all evening, then you will lose that customer. Being there for them doesn't mean literally being there for them at their shoulder: it means being there for them at a polite distance. Always read the customer's body language as carefully as you listen to their spoken language: what is their body language telling you about the level of attention they want?

"SERVICE IS...
AN EMOTIONAL TRANSACTION."

The wise Mitchell Schmieding of Trotter's restaurant really hits the nail on the head here with this most telling remark: everything in a restaurant is a transaction, but service is the one element, the connecting link between server and served, that makes the relationship an emotional experience. Without this emotional transaction, then it's no more than dinner and drinks. But with this emotional element, then suddenly we have a captivating entertainment, an idyll, and the very essence of civilisation.

"YOU WORK FOR SUCCESS, BUT IT'S THE FAILURES THAT WILL HELP YOU GET TO THE NEXT SUCCESS."

They will probably carve this quote of Charlie Trotter on his gravestone. As an aphorism about what it means to be a restaurateur, to be an all-too-fallible human person in a hugely complex and insanely demanding business, failure is what you get, mixed with the occasional success. It's a bittersweet business.

primer

• Service is not just the business of bringing food and drink to a table: it begins with how you sell your offer to an audience.

• Marketing is a part of service, and marketing is not a dirty word, it's a fact of restaurant life.

• Service is about the customer, so check your ego and your personal problems at the door.

• The food is only one of five elements of a successful restaurant (the other four being drinks, service, value, atmosphere) and all five elements are equally important.

• Good service creates loyal customers, and loyal customers should never be taken for granted.

• Great service makes sure every customer leaves happy.

• Great service means helping out in every department.

• Don't be afraid to fire difficult customers.

• Failure should be seen as a provocation as much as a problem.

• Restaurant service is the key emotional transaction between staff and customers.

• Send loyal customers a Christmas card.

6

6

"I don't believe that people go to restaurants because they're hungry. They go because they want to be together. They want the restaurant to make their dining time a harmony of balances. It's not fantasy, but the extension of reality".

JOE BAUM

HOW A ROOM WORKS

Ambience. Atmosphere. Mood. Call it whatever you will, but the feel of a restaurant room is one of the most crucial factors in ensuring the success of a restaurant. So, how do you get it right?

ATTITUDE AND LANGUAGE

"One slice or two?"

That may sound like a reasonable enough way to ask a customer how many pieces of bread they would like. If it is reasonable, it is also, however, completely wrong.

Generosity is one of the major features of a restaurant experience and one of the major ways in which staff set the mood of the room. Phrasing the question in the way illustrated above does anything but suggest generosity. It suggests meanness, and it makes the customer feel self-conscious if they ask for that second slice.

The question, then, should be rephrased as a proposition: "May I offer you some bread?" is immediately followed by "Would you like a second slice."

The rule is to follow the principle of "Je vous propose": everything you do is an offer for the customer.

In making this offer, you effectively create the atmosphere and the oasis that makes a restaurant experience work. The restaurant becomes a place where the customer is, in effect, spoilt for choice, the choice of foods, wines, service, mood.

If you do not demand the correct attitude, and if you do not set it by example for your staff, then you will fail to create a successful room, a room that – however briefly – takes the customer beyond the pressures of normal life.

And it doesn't matter that your premises may simply be a sausage sandwich shop: language dictates mood and dictates the customer's response whenever and wherever you are offering food.

In the Charlie Trotter book dealt with at length above, Kurt Sorensen, general manager of Charlie Trotter's food shop, makes this point explicitly: "We work on how we address the guests... Rather than say 'Do you want something?' when a guest walks up to the counter, we'll say 'Do you care for a taste?'. Just like in the restaurant, we think there is a gentler, more refined way of doing things."

That "gentler, more refined" way begins right at the outset, when a staff member picks up the telephone and uses their reply to begin the relationship with the customer: "Good evening, Restaurant casa de la maison chez nous, Ralph speaking, how may I help you?"

Instantly, we have a proposal "How may I help you?" from a staff member that starts the relationship on the right foot: this is the first offer to be made between restaurant and customer, and all the language used hereafter must underline the propositional philosophy on which the relationship is based.

For many restaurateurs, attitude is not something that is an aspect of atmosphere, but I would suggest it is one of the most important.

The image of the over-bearing sommelier who is determined to intimidate the customer about their wine choice is simply the classic example of how restaurants get the question of atmosphere all wrong. If the customer feels intimidated, then

AMBIENCE
je • vous • propose

you have lost them, and you have lost them because the attitude of the sommelier is all wrong.

Whilst he – it is usually a he – should be making a proposition which offers the customer the luxury of choice, he is instead doing nothing more than demonstrating superiority. No customer who is made to feel inferior will ever return.

Everything you do in creating atmosphere in a restaurant begins with generosity, and the expression of that generosity through your language. Mean people do not make successful restaurateurs, and the most successful restaurateurs are infinitely generous, and know how to express it.

UNIFORMS

Staff have to be easily and speedily delineated from customers, so choosing the correct style of uniform is vital to the feel and success of a room.

Shirts and ties and trousers and aprons, for everyone, seem to me to be a mixture that is hard to beat. From bistro to brasserie and on to a top-flight restaurant, they look good, they mark out the crew, and they are simple to launder. Just make sure that you buy durable stuff: restaurant work is all action, and flimsy attire will fall apart in weeks.

The classic style of uniform also offers to the customer an element of historical association and comfort: in our mind's eye we are all familiar with that archetypal French restaurant style, where waiters and managers look like waiters and managers.

I saw this sort of association at work one day in a fashionable

Otto Kunze. Otto's Creative Catering, Butlerstown, County Cork

As I don't like to repeat all the points of advice in this book, which I can only agree with, I want to mention a few additional thoughts:

Jane Grubb of Cashel Blue fame recently pointed out: "The secret of success is the passion for what you are doing": she refers to cheese making, I see it as vital to our trade. You have to have a passion for good cooking and for creating an atmosphere of hospitality and it has to be fun. This transfers to your customers, they feel wanted, and that you enjoy cooking for them.

When you design your place start with the thought: How would I like the atmosphere, the choice on the menu? This way you are able to create a genuine article, which comes across as unique and convincing.

Of course you can't only put on your favourite dishes but have to cater for meat and fish eaters as well as for vegetarians but don't follow fashions and silly conventions.

I hate the pre-historical style of formal, intrusive and overbearing service that seems to be a pre-condition of a Michelin star. (Once a sommelier nearly slapped my hand for trying to help myself to a glass of my wine.) In one of the "top" places (not a Michelin star, but price-wise the top end) I had an experience recently that I could summarise as "show food, not slow food".

The only good thing of a four-hour, seven-course meal was an espresso cup full of a good consommé.

If you are not in a location with a large number of potential customers passing your door every day and can thereby specialise your set up to suit a sub-culture and become exclusive of other people, then see yourself as supplying a service to your local community.

Implement an inclusive strategy by catering for different tastes and treat "normal" people the same as the VIPs that bring you corporate business.

Be an active member of your local community, employ locals, shop locally, support local activities and charities. Give cookery demonstration to the ICA or in local schools. If your neighbours know and respect you and if you give them good food and value for money, you have regulars all year round. They do the advertising for you and direct visitors to you.

A short cut is the sure way to failure: Never serve food that is not in top condition. Only buy in products that you can trace yourself to the producer. I don't trust the existing government quality assurance schemes; they define quality only by means of HACCP compliance; that means non toxic. I only serve quality, defined as tasty, wholesome and healthy and not highly processed: that stuff is only good for the shareholders of the likes of Kerry Foods.

Never take on more customers than your staffing level and your available food allows. Define you "booked out level' not only

AMBIENCE
je • vous • propose

according to your seating capacity, but to the number of customers you can serve satisfactorily.

Some restaurateurs see Environmental Health Officers as a hazard to their own health; they could induce a heart attack or drive you to drink. This is the wrong approach. The Food Safety Authority is on the same side as we are: we don't want to poison our customers, but have them come back and tell all their friends about the experience. I see the EHO as a support in a case of a bogus food poisoning claim and I was assured of a procedure in place that follows these up. In a case of alleged poisoning, I would ring up my EHO immediately and ask the customer to get in touch with a doctor and the EHO to clarify the situation.

Most requirements in regards of layout of food preparation areas are a great help, like knee-operated hand wash basins with paper dispensers attached; fly screens; plenty of dedicated wash basins; easy to clean non slip flooring; stainless steel or PVC wall covering. But you hear stories of young EHO's who unfortunately know rules and regulations, but nothing about good food. Some show culinary expertise, not exceeding easy singles and pot noodles, and tend to turn

green when you enthusiastically refer to raw egg mayonnaise, steak tartare or sushi. Sadly no work experience in various types of food businesses is yet part of their qualification. Some apply regulations for high-volume food processing units with the high risk factors as in unskilled and unmotivated workers at minimum wages, to your proprietor/chef run operation.

Don't be afraid of them when they cover their insecurity (and their backside, as true civil servants) by unreasonable demands and bullying. Stand your ground firmly (but politely) and demand a meeting with the next superior. The higher up the ladder, the more common sense can be found. Talk to other restaurateurs and exchange experiences. Don't follow the EHO's blind trust in paperwork and chemicals. Elbow grease and plain liquid soap cleans best. The disinfectant chemicals and their residues are pure poison.

Finally: Don't expect to get rich fast. Be prudent with bank loans and leases. Overheads are huge and it takes a while to get established. The higher the quality of food and service, the lower the profit margin.

If you are only in it for the money, buy a chipper.

Dublin restaurant. One of the country's leading media personalities left his table to go to the bathroom. He was wearing a white shirt, black trousers and a dark-coloured tie. As he made his way across the dining room floor, a female customer looked up from her lunch and instinctively called out, "Excuse me, waiter..." The media star died a million deaths.

Of course, with a funkier, younger style of room, you may want to have the Diesel jeans and the Wagamama-style T-shirts so that the staff can show just how hip they are. The only rule is to try to have some consistency, otherwise things become too confusing for the customer. One aspect of uniform that is frequently overlooked is footwear. People in restaurants eat up mileage on a shift, so comfortable, flat shoes are a must.

MUSIC

Miles Davis' classic album, *Kind of Blue* is a favourite standby for restaurateurs. A timeless sextet date from 1959 that featured other legendary jazzers such as Bill Evans and John Coltrane, the work is respected as a pioneering example of modal jazz.

Much more importantly, however, it is revered as one of the most mellifluously moody jazz records of all time: right after that cymbal shimmers at the end of the opening statement of *So What*, you are captivated in Miles Davis' intricate soundscape.

I introduced this disc, along with some other jazz stuff including Davis' splendid recording, *Cookin*, to the staff at one consultancy project. It all worked a treat in making the room feel sexy, sophisticated, hip. The manager got the jazz bug, and went out to get some more Miles Davis stuff. One of the discs he selected was called *Big Fun*. Sounds perfect. Big night out. Big fun. A match made in heaven.

Except it was a match made in hell. *Big Fun* is described in Richard Cook and Brian Morton's splendid Penguin *Guide to*

AMBIENCE
je • vous • propose

Jazz as enjoying a "sudden, alienating wallop..." whilst simultaneously featuring "a distorted, almost pain-racked trumpet, the dissonant bleat of soprano saxophone, electric keyboards, thumping, funk-laden bass and a great slew of percussion".

That's right: *Big Fun* can empty a room in about 40 seconds flat. If you wanted to scare people with a single record, it is a good place to start. Follow it up with Captain Beefheart's *Trout Mask Replica* and you should manage to evacuate your entire street.

The lesson is simple: good music works brilliantly to create mood, but the wrong music will have exactly the opposite effect.

So, what is the key? The answer is rhythm. Rhythm in music helps people to relax. It sets mood, it contributes colour. It is precisely because of this that jazz works so well in many restaurant spaces. The rhythm becomes the predominant factor in what people hear.

Because it must also be said that music which people are too conscious of in a restaurant can be a problem, a distraction. You should sense the music even more than you should hear it. The rhythm should help people to feel relaxed, whilst the voices and instruments should not distract them.

Another factor that is important to consider is familiarity. If rhythm helps people to relax, so does the familiar sound of a well-known piece of music. Your customers may not know that they know *Kind of Blue*, but they do: as perhaps the most familiar jazz of the last 45 years, it is a small part of all our consciousness.

As such, we react subliminally to it: it is pleasing, and so we find it relaxing. This subliminal reaction is important, and the music should have the same notes of familiarity as the menu, the wine list and the behaviour of the service. Put these subliminal triggers together, and you have a very happy customer.

But, you cannot play Miles Davis all day long, so what else works? Mozart is the most sublimely rhythmical classical composer, and as such Wolfgang's music is perfect for mornings and lunchtimes. In fact, no other composer's music is anywhere near so relaxing to the human soul. The sort of classical music that fails is, however, one of the most frequently played: operatic arias. You may have an inordinate fondness for Andrea Bocelli, but I would advise that you keep it a private matter. Operatic arias are all about crescendo, and crescendo is the enemy of mood.

This is one reason why playing current pop music so often fails: after three minutes, there is another belt of chirpy sound syrup distracting you from your dinner. Once, when checking out of a fine hotel in County Mayo, I praised the proprietor for a job well done, whilst pointing out that the music let down everything else about the carefully considered dining room. "Oh, but my husband just hits the 'random' button on the CD player every evening", she explained.

Exactly: if you go for random, you abolish mood. Music must be considered, otherwise it will undermine your best efforts at creating mood.

There is another school of thought regarding music, however. For some restaurateurs, their choice of music is as much of a statement as the choice of food on their menus. If you hear Miles Davis' *Bitches Brew* in Dublin's Mermaid Café, or Sheila

AMBIENCE
je • vous • propose

Chandra in Cork's Ivory Tower, or the engagingly strange Stina Nordenstam in Dublin's Halo, then you are listening to sound as style, not sound as mood.

The music in these restaurants is a vital part of the package, and whilst I applaud it, I also recognise that it is exceedingly difficult to strike this personal manifesto at just the right pitch. The staff may get a kick out of listening to Stina Nordenstam, and it may just be that the customers are as hip as the staff and also enjoy Stina's curious lickle girlie voice. But, chances are there are some customers grating their teeth.

This use of sound reaches its nadir when a restaurant plays the newest release of some pop star or other, just because it is new, and irrespective of whether it suits the room or not. If you want to listen to your favourite popstar, get an i-Pod and keep your fandom to yourself.

Here are a dozen who don't work:

Arnold Schoenberg, and his pupils. Nirvana. Dmitri Shostakovich. Queens of the Stone Age. Andrea Bocelli. Neil Young. Leonard Cohen. Tom Waits. Alfred Schnittke. John Coltrane. Radiohead. John Zorn

And a dozen who do:

Miles Davis (up to 1965). Wolfgang Amadeus Mozart. Bill Evans. Dizzy Gillespie. Ella Fitzgerald. Sam Cooke. Bebil Gilberto. Underworld. Hildegard of Bingen. Frank Sinatra (Capitol Records period). Charlie Parker. Duke Ellington.

DESIGN

"GOD GAVE THE IRISH THE GIFT OF FRIENDSHIP. UNFORTUNATELY, HE ALSO MADE THEM BLIND."

I first heard this remark back in the late 1980's, and it has troubled me ever since. Are the Irish a visually illiterate people? I don't think so. And if we are, no one has told David Collins.

I think what we lack, which is what you would expect of a people who until recently have been rural rather than urban dwellers, is a nous when it comes to design; if we designate design as the ability to put the right object in the right place.

Irish restaurants are full of the right design objects, sitting in the wrong place. Knowing when something is in its rightful place is a skill that eludes many restaurateurs, and it is only when you see the work of those gifted people who have "the eye" that you realise how so many others get it all wrong.

And a successful, workable, functioning design is vital for success. If a room is badly designed, it will not feel right: its feng shui will be bad and, without knowing it, people will not feel comfortable in the room, which means they will not return.

They are likely not to be so explicit about it, but they will know that something about the room is not relaxing, and so they are not relaxed. You may very well have spent a gazillion euro on design, but if it doesn't work to make people feel comfortable, then you will fail. Good design creates comfort, whether it is minimalist, maximalist, or just some work of bricolage thrown together by yourself out of odds and ends.

AMBIENCE
je • vous • propose

So, what to do? Firstly, recognise your limitations. If you don't have the eye that automatically tells you where to put something, then get a designer, and get a designer who will work with you. The sort of autocrat who comes into a project with their mind made up will only result in disaster. You need someone who will visualise your ideas, and take them further, and who will work within budget. Designer and client must work harmoniously.

If you have the budget, then paying top dollar for David Collins or some other icon restaurant designer will be money well spent. Great designers can not only create great rooms, they can transform rooms that are disaster zones: the work by Arthur Gibney on The Cellar Restaurant in Dublin's Merrion Hotel is testament to what a great designer can do with a room that was virtually a no-go zone.

Similarly, the flamboyant design of Halo restaurant in The Morrison Hotel by John Rocha is one of the key signatures of that destination address.

But, this all costs a lot of money, and there is another way. Opting for a particularly personal, particularly idiosyncratic design can be just as successful.

Think of some of the great dining rooms in the country – O'Callaghan-Walshe in Roscarbery; Allo's Bar in Listowel; Buggy's Glencairn Inn; La Marine in Rosslare, Coast in Tramore, The Mermaid Café in Dublin – and you quickly realise that what makes them work is the pell-mell unpredictability of the style, the wilful individuality of these rooms.

But, what also makes them work is the fact that the right things are in the right place: the feng shui of all these rooms is just right, they are destination addresses where you want to stay because they make you feel good.

It is not easy to achieve this: for every Coast or O'Callaghan-Walshe, there are half a dozen places that don't manage to create such a successful design mood. In fact, there are a dozen places that don't manage to create such a successful design mood. So, let's have a few outline rules:

1. MIX THE CONTEMPORARY WITH THE CLASSIC

If your design is too far-out, people will not feel comfortable, as their expectations of what a restaurant space should be are not being met. Remember that no matter how minimalist or avant garde your design, you are fundamentally aiming to create a comfort zone where people can relax. This doesn't demand that you spend a lot of money, and wind up creating some preposterous baroque bordello, but simply that you think carefully about mixing the old and the new.

2. MAKE IT FLEXIBLE

Or, to put it simply, you can't put two circular tables together, so work out a design that can adapt to groups large and small, and which can be changed at speed in case you have a sudden booking for a group who want to eat before the theatre, which then only allows you ten minutes to change the room before evening service.

3. MAKE SURE IT WORKS FOR THE STAFF AS WELL AS THE CUSTOMERS

Customers hate tables that are too close together, but staff hate them even more. Again, the rule is comfort: what is comfortable for customers will also be comfortable for the staff.

4. ALWAYS KEEP NATURAL LIGHT

A friend had some tenants developing a building into a restaurant. "Would you ever take a quick look at what they're doing?" he asked me, so I did.

I arrived just when the builders were about to lower an entire ceiling at the back of the room, thus blocking out the light from a large ceiling window. Had they lowered the ceiling and lost the light, they would have created a room that was, in effect, a large tunnel.

People do not like tunnels. Tunnels are scary, repellent. Any moviemaker or novelist who wants to put the heeby-jeebies up us just has to film or describe a tunnel scene, and already we are squirming with terror.

Natural light also acts as an attraction, simply because people are drawn to it. Watch what happens when people enter a room: they will inevitably and predictably gravitate to the window seats like moths to a flame. Natural light gives comfort, so always seek to maximise it.

And, of course, it saves on your electricity bills.

primer

• Using the correct language is a vital part of creating an atmosphere that makes people relax in a restaurant.

• Direct all your actions into making a proposition to the customer: je vous propose.

• Staff need uniforms which make them instantly identifiable by customers. They also need flat shoes.

• Music creates mood through rhythm and familiarity. Consider the sounds carefully, and never hit the "random" button on the CD player.

• If you don't have an eye for design, hire someone who does. Otherwise, don't be afraid to be idiosyncratic.

• Design has to work for staff as well as customers.

• Always use as much natural light as possible.

7

7

"The bottle and the meal completed, it would leave a profound digestive calm. A spiritual calm, too, as if the wine had lifted the meal from out of the rattle of daily repetition, glazing it with a sudden, Zen-like benediction."

ANDREW JEFFORD

WRITING A WINE LIST

Wine lists present one of the great opportunities to intrigue and stimulate your customers, yet for the most part, restaurateurs appear content to allow them to be dull, uninformative, and characterless.

For some restaurateurs, this happens because their interest in wine is marginal, so they will simply not bother to create a wine list, they will actually allow one supplier to both supply the wines and write the wine list.

This is a disastrous thing to do. Firstly, the list will simply be a configuration of wine-speak clichés that will tell you nothing about the wines, and, secondly, the list will not be interesting, far less intriguing. Like delivery-docket menus, single-supplier wine lists are evidence of simple laziness. Needless to say, the two are frequently to be found in the one place.

So, what should a wine list actually do? What are the elements that should intrigue and excite the customer?

I think a good list does something very basic: it tells you about the place the wine comes from, it tells you about the person who made it, and it gives some idea of what it is like to drink and the sort of food that it pairs with. If you can add in a little human interest story, then so much the better.

Here is the sort of thing I mean:

Clos d'Yvigne, Princesse de Cleves Sauvignon Blanc, Bergerac, France 1999

Patricia Atkinson moved to France from England more than a decade ago, and makes this lush sauvignon in Bergerac, east of Bordeaux. We think Patricia has a better handle on what to do with sauvignon than any native Bordelais.

What have we got? A female winemaker, still a rarity, but more than that, we have a transplanted Englishwoman making wine in the heartland of France, close to Bordeaux.

She is working with a classic variety - sauvignon blanc – which she makes in a rich, lush style, and the writer gets cheeky enough to assert that she could teach the natives a thing or two.

What's missing? Well, a quote from a reputable wine writing source is always good: "Tim Atkin of *The Observer* has suggested Patricia's wines can equal the status of classed growth Bordeaux" might finish the description off nicely.

Person. Place. Product. And, don't forget, Personality. The Personality is yours: a list works when you can hear an authorial voice, when you can hear someone's passion and prejudices. If you have a big thing about Riesling, for instance, then feature the wines, and describe why you are so keen on them.

But, remember this simple rule: every wine on the list has to be there for a reason. This is why suppliers' lists don't work: those wines are only there because the supplier ships them. What you want to achieve is a situation where every wine on the list has good reason to be there, either because you are so fond of it, or because it offers such splendid value, or because it goes particularly well with your style of food.

And if the wine does all these three things, then spell it out: "Former ballet dancer and wing-forward Bruce Corkhat makes this rollocking Shiraz in the Barossa Valley in south Australia. Bruce must have had our Tipperary sirloin in mind when he was dancing on the grapes, and the super-keen price makes it a real treat."

They know how to do this sort of thing particularly well in

WINE
person • place • product

Belfast. Here is how Jonathan Davis, of Alden's Restaurant, does it:

Domaine de L'Hortus Grande Cuvée 1997, Pic St. Loup, Languedoc, France

The special cuvée from one of Southern France's most highly regarded estates. A blend of grenache, syrah, mourvedre and cinsault. If you want to try something new, you can't go wrong with this.

That is textbook wine list writing, save that the name of the winemaker could be added, something Mr Davis does with many of the wines on a fabulous list.

Here is how the masterly veteran Nick Price, of Nick's Warehouse, does it:

Wolf Blass Shiraz President's Selection 1998 South Australia

I could sit and sniff this wine, close my eyes and imagine that I'm in a blackberry thicket. A treat!

Mr Price has the experience and confidence, not to mention the wit, to break almost all the rules. His notes are entirely personal, and entirely seductive: you want that bottle, now!

Wine lists also work best when they are reasonably short. In Charlie Trotter's, dealt with in detail elsewhere in this book, they hand you a 55-page list. That is crazy: no one has the time to wade through such an extensive list, and for many people that sort of bulk is simply going to be intimidating.

You are much better to have a short list of hand-chosen wines, tasted by you and the staff, vintage after vintage, and about which you are informed and critical. You wouldn't offer someone a 55-page menu, so why should the wine list be a blockbuster? Ideally, menus and wine lists should be much the same length: both should be capable of being taken in by the customer with one look.

And, as you write and rewrite the menu, you should be doing something similar with the wine list, adding notes and newspaper quotes, adding new vintages, making changes according to supplies. There is nothing worse than the leather-bound wine list, with its contents slipped in between plastic sheets, that looks and feels as if it has never changed. The style of the offer is vital: get it right, write it right, and you will provoke the customer to choose something interesting.

And there is no need to follow the conventional fashion in wine lists. In the consultancy project from which the Clos d'Yvigne wine example above was part of the wine list, we came up with these criteria for choosing, listing and describing wines:

Classics -

handpicked examples of Sancerre, Chablis, Châteauneuf-du-Pape and Fleurie.

Wine 2 Ways -

where we featured a Riesling from New Zealand alongside an Alsatian Riesling.

We Love South-West France -

a chance to feature some of the favoured wines of the manager from that zone.

Great Discoveries -

part of the list we could change in order to include wines discovered at new tastings.

WINE
person • place • product

The Female Touch -

Wines made by women, which is where Patricia Atkinson's wines came in.

Contemporary Friends -

which allowed us to pick quirky wines that were out of the norm.

A Happy Couple -

where we put two contrasting wines by the same winemaker together.

and we concluded with Pudding Wines and Bubbly.

In total, we used less than thirty wines, but arranging them into such unorthodox categories was a great success, and attracted a great deal of attention.

A concise list also makes it much easier to educate the staff about the wines they are selling, and educating the staff is vital, and fun, and gives them a real feeling of involvement and participation.

How do you educate them? Tasting, is the simple answer. The winemaker Johnny Hugel once told me: never open a book on wine until you have tried 300 different bottles.

That is sound advice: there is much to be learnt from some of the great wine writers such as Andrew Jefford or Oz Clarke or Jancis Robinson or Patrick Matthews, but there is no substitute for tasting, because only then can you get a true sense of the real nature of the wine.

Tasting will reveal the character and quirkiness of a wine, showing you its texture, for instance; a vital consideration when making a wine suggestion to accompany dishes on the menu; and its potency, something to be seriously considered in this age of high-alcohol wines.

And you use the wine books, then, to fill in the geographical information, the deep background, to tell you who is working where. And, when it comes to writing the list, remember that it is your personality, and not meaningless wine-speak, that must come through. You picked the bottle, so you must be its advocate, both in words and deeds. If you respect the wine and the winemaker, then tell people in words and deeds. For everyone loves a new wine discovery.

What's more, once staff are enthusiastic and informed about the wines, they will do a much better job of selling them for you. Selling wine is often a matter of being prepared to offer an enthusiastic suggestion to a slightly hesitant customer, and this sort of emotional engagement is vital for a successful relationship between staff and customer.

And, if a customer says a wine is corked or tainted, never argue, simply take it back. The chances are that they are right:

"THIS IS ONE OF FRITZ'S JOKES: 'DID YOU HEAR ABOUT THE RESTAURANT ON THE MOON? GREAT FOOD. NO ATMOSPHERE'."

ALICE WATERS, FANNY AT CHEZ PANISSE

the extent of corked bottles is unfortunately quite high, and you should be looking out for this when you pull the cork: always give it a sniff.

And do look out for a table where people are not finishing their wine, as many people lack the nerve to decide that a wine is corked, and will simply toy with it and suffer in silence as it ruins their food, rather than sending it back. If you can sort that out discreetly and sympathetically, you will make a loyal customer. If they are wrong - and they have simply chosen a style of wine they decide they don't like - then never make an issue of it, because you will not persuade them to drink it.

Finally, don't sell wines that are available in shops and supermarkets. People will compare prices, which will make you look mean. Be unique, and start enjoying those 300 bottles.

primer

• Don't buy wines from a single supplier, and don't let a supplier write your wine list.

• The key information to impart in a wine list is: who makes the wine, where do they make it, and what do they make it from? Person. Place. Product.

• There is no ideal structure for a wine list: write it according to how you see fit.

• Every wine on the list has to have a good reason to be there.

• Let your own personality come through in the descriptions of the wines, but don't try writing either a novel or a manifesto: wine lists should be confined to information, not opinion or anecdote.

• Keep the list concise and simple, both in the range of wines and in the way you describe them. And don't lapse into "wine-speak".

• Keep changing, annotating and revising your list, treat it just as you would treat your menus.

• Staff must know their wines intimately, and knowing them will help them sell wine to customers.

• Sample 300 different bottles in order to really understand the world of wine. Start today.

Tom O'Connell, O'Connell's Restaurant, Ballsbridge, Dublin

10 THINGS YOU NEED TO KNOW TO RUN A RESTAURANT SUCCESSFULLY:

1. Knowledge of food
2. Common sense, common sense sales & marketing, common sense purchasing
3. Leadership and human relations skills
4. Reasonable administrative skills
5. A good accountant
6. How to work smart – planning, organising, controlling
7. Empathy - ability to read what the customer wants
8. Knowledge of safe food, health & safety and other statutory requirements
9. How to train
10. How to network

If you had all these skills perfectly honed as one person, you would not be running a successful restaurant, you would own all the restaurants in town!

The first and most important thing to do is to look in the mirror and own up to yourself. What are you good at and what do you need to "farm out". In my view the 10 skills listed above are essential to having a successful business. One of the biggest mistakes we restaurateurs make is to think that we are running a restaurant with all the creativity and romance that entails. Stop Now! You are running firstly a BUSINESS and secondly a restaurant. We get all consumed by the product, the uniqueness of our offer and put the bottom-line on the long finger. This is why many in our number are "busy fools".

I was recently shocked to sit with one of Ireland's greats and listen to the tale of a business from which that person has now retired. On retiring and having sold the business, there was little left. No pension, little capital and, suddenly, no life – the business had been that person's life! There is something wrong here. This had been a destination restaurant, a "known" person of the trade, a great host, yet the person retired with little. If this story does not make us sit up, what will?

What is the moral of this story? "Look after Number One". If your business cannot guarantee your present and your future, get out now!

Usually your accountant will see the light before you do. It is, therefore, worthwhile to include in the initial brief to your accountant: "if the need arises, tell me when to get out".

1. KNOWLEDGE OF FOOD

The creator of McDonalds must have liked a good burger. I expect the Pratt family of Avoca like good food. Myrtle Allen of Ballymaloe will talk at length about new season's potatoes and the farmer who always has good potatoes. Aidan McManus and Terry McCoy are passionate about their fish and are regularly found on the quay. Finally, I expect newcomer Domini Kemp of Itsabagel loves New York's best bagels.

These are some of the greats of the food business who keep their fingers "on the pulse".

Bill Clinton famously said "it's the economy stupid! " In our business we can add "it's the food stupid!"

Somehow I feel that one of the key "must knows" is your food.

However, when you do your purchasing consider that your accountant is sitting on one shoulder and your bank manager on the other. There is no point in having the freshest turbot in Ireland on the menu if your customer is only willing to pay for lemon sole.

Our food experience at O'Connell's is – give the customer the food they want, at the price they want to pay and they will return in droves.

2. COMMON SENSE, COMMON SENSE MARKETING, COMMON SENSE PURCHASING

Success stories abound of people who "never sat the Leaving Certificate" making it big in business. The restaurant business is no exception.

I believe that basic common sense is an essential to success. This goes from the principle of location, location, location to remaining ultra alert to the changing desires of your target customer and buying your raw materials at the correct price.

As to marketing, there are big businesses who say that you must spend a minimum of 4% on marketing. Then you must aim at a bottom line of say 6%. Who in our business spends 4% on marketing or, indeed, 0.4%? Therefore, there is a need to be creative, to be a good networker and to use public relations effectively.

There are so many ways other than expensive marketing. For me the most effective and least expensive marketing is done each moment the restaurant is open. How? …… by ensuring your product is perfect, all of the time, every time; delicious, consistent, correctly priced, delivered as part of an overall "pleasant, must-repeat experience".

Our experience in O'Connell's has been

as such. We have relied totally on the quality of our product to market. When our product has been at its best in every respect, our business has prospered. The Carlsberg advertisement comes to mind. A disused marketing department - an empty office.

If there is "magic on the plate" and in the delivery of the customer's expectation then you can forget the need to devote huge amounts of time to formal marketing strategies. You will have the least expensive and the most successful marketing of all - word of mouth.

Equally when our product weakened for whatever reason (if I had not "woken-up" to it myself), the profit and loss statement would be showing it within four weeks.

In all countries the local press and guide writers are powerful in influencing restaurant choice. They operate on word of mouth – they come, they take a snap shot, write and publish. For me the moral is: you have got to be perfect always and if you get a bad write-up it's only correct. After all, you've charged good money and the consumer, or in this case the journalist/writer, deserves the promised good experience.

We do actually spend money on four mediums @ O'Connell's:

• Advertising on our two local bus shelters "turns on the tap". Better value than a three second glance on the back page of a prestigious paper – on the bus shelters you are "up" for two weeks and if it's "catchy" the message gets directly home to your daily drive-by market.

• A web site – kept up-to-date;

• The Ryanair website;

• The *Dining in Dublin* menu book – sold through bookshops and newsagents and placed in most of Dublin's hotel bedrooms.

A small business cannot afford a huge marketing budget but must have a great product. I tell our top chefs and front of house people that they are the marketing department.

Finally to purchasing – every cent spent in purchasing of raw materials is spent forever and is 100% out of profits. It is essential to seek out great produce at the best price. Produce at a price that allows you to be a profitable business. We are a sizeable business and can negotiate on volume. I strongly believe that smaller restaurants in one area should group their purchases. Then in partnership with suppliers, better purchase prices could be achieved by helping the suppliers to also cut costs – by one weekly delivery, etc.

3. LEADERSHIP & HUMAN RELATIONS SKILLS

I once attended a talk given by the famous Gaelic footballer/manager Mick O'Dwyer. He was speaking about team building. He spoke of the need to have "the ability to engender in people the willingness to convert passion to action and, subsequently, winning results."

You've got to be a good leader, know how to put a team together and manage it for the good of individuals and for the business.

You've also got to hire to that team, positions and individuals who compensate for your own weaknesses. If you hate administration then you must have a good administrator on board. If you are an introvert, then put an extrovert into the team. In our business the customers want interaction.

Evolve together targets, expectations, strategies, a mission statement and so on – so that everyone is working to the same end.

Regular daily ("morning prayers"), weekly, monthly and annual planning meetings are a must. A level of formality appropriate to your own style is essential. Have records (can be as simple as a hard covered book) of these meetings so that targets are achieved and problems are "closed-out".

4. REASONABLE ADMINISTRATIVE SKILLS

Very often the "professionals" in our business are "creatives" and, therefore, not the best administrators. It is absolutely essential to recognise your personal strengths and weaknesses and, as mentioned previously, hire people to cover your weaknesses. Have people who thrive on the area in which you are weak or "hate doing".

5. A GOOD ACCOUNTANT

Without a good accountant (out-sourced and/ or a cost accountant in-house) the business is like a boat lost at sea.

Have financial reporting by meal period, the day, the week, the month, the quarter, the year.

It's just down to the basics – the smallest business can be financially managed if you use the KISS system. Keep it simple stupid! After all it's just sales (please, always net of VAT), less costs that makes profit or loss.

A few copybooks, binders and a hole punch, with a minimum of discipline will keep a small place on the straight and narrow – but you've got to do it.

If you involve your people they will do it for you - delegate at every level.

6. WORK SMART

PLAN
- Know where you want to get to
- Have a budget and sales forecasts

- Plan actions that will influence sales
- Plan staffing requirements
- Plan your premises to produce at optimum cost levels

ORGANISE

- Efficiency will reduce costs
- Have the best people you can afford
- Be organised at every level of the business

CONTROL

- Check, check and check again at every level:
- Financial results
- Product quality and delivery
- Convert complaints to friends
- Staff and customer satisfaction
- Cost levels – root out "hidden costs"
- Waste

DELEGATE

We are all guilty of carrying the world on our shoulders. Reflect when you sign off the weekly wages as to why you are working like a slave and paying out such a large amount in wages.

Reflect on how to get better use from that weekly outlay.

Most employees will rise to the challenge of a more fulfilling role. They will not necessarily want more pay for the small extra tasks that will make all the difference to the efficiency of the business.

7. EMPATHY

I firmly believe in the need for a good dose

of empathy on the part of any business person, not least a restaurateur.

You've got to have empathy with your guests and your staff.
What do your customers want?
Why are they choosing your restaurant?
Are they celebrating, are they happy, unhappy, joyful, mourning, excited?
Whatever the mood, you've got to deliver to that occasion.

Not only is it enough to pick up on the vibes – you've got to act on them.
I regularly make very profound decisions on the business based principally on interaction and empathy with our customers.

The very same applies to your team of management and employees.

8. KNOWLEDGE OF SAFE FOOD, HEALTH & SAFETY AND ALL STATUTORY REQUIREMENTS

If you don't know yourself, get a competent consultant to guide you.

Be meticulous in the pursuit and achievement of best practice.

Be ruthless in acting on persistent non-conformance to any statutory requirements in your business.

9. HOW TO TRAIN

Training is everything.
It is how you get things done your way.
It is how best practice is converted from words to consistent delivery.

Training, in my view, is my personal assurance that the business will perform to the standards and results to which we aspire.

A minimum "structure" must be put in place. Statutory training must be achieved.

Every business in the world has dusty shelves with marvellous manuals created by marvellous people. These creators were duly promoted because of the marvellous manual they created. However, it (the manual) never got off the shelf!

My view is: Keep the text brief, up-to-date and accurate. Ensure daily as well as weekly training. Make training part of the normal day. As the chef prepares food before the restaurant opens, each department should have a period of training as an integral part of the day.

Have dedicated trainers in each area and have a formal training review with a weekly or meeting monthly. Make key people accountable for training.

10. HOW TO NETWORK

Networking is important as much with industry colleagues as with other business people in your area.

Try to be part of the local community in a way in which you personally are comfortable.

In Ireland people have a great sense of community. When "the chips are down" your involvement in your community will be your strength.

"THE FINEST BUTTER AND LOTS OF TIME."

FERNAND POINT

8

8

"We all believed in community and personal commitment and quality. Chez Panisse was born out of these ideals. Profit was always secondary."

ALICE WATERS

VALUE

Value is not the same as cost. Value for money is a perception, yet another of those amorphous ideas which are difficult to quantify, but which successful restaurants seem to accomplish almost with ease.

People will happily pay high prices for food and wine, so long as they feel they are getting value for money. But the line that separates the feeling of value from the feeling of being ripped off is very slender indeed: charging 20 cent too much can alienate a customer who would not think twice about adding 20 euro to a bill for service if they feel they have been well looked after.

Value is yet another of those comfort zones that make people feel secure and happy in a restaurant. With all the other essential elements, value for money brings people back to a restaurant and, for those places which can appear to over-deliver on value, the resulting success can be enormous.

Perhaps the finest example of this was the extraordinary success of Roly's Bistro, in Dublin's Ballsbridge, during the 1990's. Never mind that Roly's did enormous numbers: their secret was that they did enormous numbers of repeat business, and that is the goal.

So, how do you make value work for you and for the customer?

A LITTLE, AND OFTEN

If you run an informal, accessible place, you should set yourself the target of getting people to visit and spend money about 20 times a year.

That doesn't mean that they are going to be in for dinner every two-and-a-half weeks. What it means is that there is some part of your offer that they can buy into, at either a high level – a celebratory, blow-out dinner – or at a lesser level – a quick working lunch, Sunday brunch with the family, picking up dinner-to-go on a mid-week evening.

The key factor to their returning so often, apart from the fact that you are doing the job well and that they like what you do, is that they are happy with what they have to spend at each point. So there must be balance between all your pricing: a cup of coffee must appear to them to be value for money, but so must your house champagne.

MAKE MONEY SLOWLY

I once shared a platform at a catering college demonstration with Ireland's most garlanded chef, Kevin Thornton of Thomton's Restaurant, Dublin.

I talked about being a critic, whilst Mr Thornton cooked some typically adventurous and intricate food for the audience of educators and students.

As Kevin finished one dish – he was cooking some mallard which had been "shot by a friend", and a second dish featured rod-caught sea bass – and just at the point when he was applying some gold leaf, one member of the audience asked the question that probably at least half the people watching were thinking.

"Kevin, could you give us any idea of what the cost of this dish would be, what the portion cost would be?"

VALUE
retail • rooms • reputation

"No idea", said Thornton.

"But if you don't know how much it costs, how will you know if you are making any money?"

"I'm not worried about making money", replied Thornton. "I'll make money in the future. I don't worry about that now".

Now, most of the people in the room probably thought Kevin Thornton was completely crazy. But, of course, he wasn't: he was right.

If you want to make a reputation, you cannot also make a lot of money from the outset.

If you are concerned solely about bottom-line, then you will never be as successful as you want to be. People know when you are out to get every last cent out of them: they can smell it, and they don't like the smell.

In answering the creative urge to cook, in answering the creative demand to be respected for what you do, you have to go back to some pretty old ideas, such as: learning your craft; serving your time; paying your dues; biding your time. Those ideas are out of fashion nowadays, but for great restaurateurs, they are as resonant with meaning as ever.

Don't be distracted by the instant celebrity which today's media offers to so many people, including those who cook for a living. Being respected as a cook – as a creative, original individual with a distinct signature style – is not the same thing as being a celebrity who happens to cook for a living.

The celebs will have their 15 minutes of fame, they will likely make lots of money, but food lovers will talk about Alice Waters and George Perry-Smith and Myrtle Allen for centuries. Reputations have to be earned: they can't be bought.

So, whilst you must make money, you should be content to make money slowly, which is to say: make a reputation, then let your reputation make money for you.

EVERYTHING IS FOR SALE

You can sleep in some hotels and, after you have checked out, you can buy the bed. And the sheets, the pillowcases, the robe, the toiletries, the whatever takes your fancy. Hotels have realised that in offering you an idyll, that there might be a part of that idyll you want to take home with you.

Fine, they say, and you stump up, and they deliver. They have maximised the customer's spend, and the customer is all the happier for it.

Why don't more restaurants do this? You have a great reputation for petits fours? So, sell them in neat little boxes so the customers can give them to someone as a gift. You are a fish restaurant? Sell the wet fish from a counter. You source piquillo peppers from Spain into which you pipe some smooth *brandade de morue* made with your own salted fish? Sell the peppers by the jar, and sell the brandade whilst you are at it.

Life, for cash-rich, time-poor people, is too short to make *brandade de morue*. And life, for the restaurateur, is too short not to maximise your customer's spend, whether it be *brandade de morue* or anything else a customer might like to buy.

As you are selling dinner, you should also be selling: a range of products produced by your kitchen; breads from your kitchen; products used in your own dishes; cooked food to go; specially selected wines that people might want to buy; tableware and any other distinctive design details that customers might throw their eye on. And take it as far as you can: I once ate at a funky restaurant in Stockholm which told us, on the menu, that the staff wore Diesel jeans. So, sell them. Or at least sell some funky Diesel aprons.

And sell the art on the wall. I have to confess that at least two of the paintings in my house were bought in restaurants, at the end of particularly enjoyable evenings. So, contact local painters, and arrange ever-changing exhibitions, and get your art for free whilst simultaneously becoming a patron of artists.

What I am proposing is that any restaurant views itself more as an emporium, and less as a single-concept destination. The mixture between cooked food destination, food-to-go-traiteur, food shop and specialist retailer is logical, and profitable.

Above all, it is synergistic: you are maximising the reach of your food products, and you are selling customers something they want to make their idyll last a little longer, whether it is simply a superb single-estate olive oil or a cookery book, or a painting. Think of the words of New York restaurateur Joe Baum, quoted elsewhere in this book, that a restaurant is "the extension of reality". By extending your customer's reality, you also extend your own financial reality.

A BEAUTIFUL BAR

People like stylish, relaxed bars, but too many restaurants either separate the function of the bar from the dining area, or else don't bother with a bar at all.

But people love to be in a bar before dinner, even if the bar happens to be across the street from the restaurant. One of the great USP's of the famous Annie's Restaurant, in Ballydehob, West Cork, is that when you walk in the door, Annie gives you the menus, and you then go back out the door and take the menus with you, across the street to Nan and Julia Levis's Bar.

Annie then comes across to take your order after you have ordered drinks and had a chance to decide what you would like to eat, and she comes a third time to fetch you for dinner.

And what do customers make of this ad hoc arrangement? They love it to bits, as the testimonials from the rich and famous from around the world that line the walls in Levis's bar testify. Mind you, I suspect that the founders of Apple and the other business and media barons who have felt moved to write letters of thanks back to Nan and Julia have probably never been in a bar where you can buy a tin of Bird's custard powder along with your gin 'n' tonic. Now that is a USP.

They also used to do something similar in the Elephant & Castle in Dublin, simply because there was no space for people to wait. One of the most elegant solutions I ever saw to the question was in a Parisian brasserie, Julien's, where a small bar was permanently thronged with people drinking kir and champagne as they waited for a table to be ready.

Waiting in a bar, therefore, is not the same as waiting. It becomes part of the experience, part of the idyll, a bar adds a dynamic to a room, it creates energy, and it makes money. It has to make money: don't think of it simply as an add-on: the bar has to deliver on the bottom line, and it will do this by serving excellent drinks prepared by skilled bartenders.

And rather than having your staff under pressure, a good, well-run bar can take pressure off a busy service.

If everyone turns up at 8pm – and everyone always turns up at 8pm! – then a bar will allow you to cope with the rush smoothly. It will also allow you to make that extra sale to a willing customer, and once that customer has had a good cocktail, they are much, much easier to deal with.

And, strangely enough, very many people who would look closely at the price of a dinner menu wouldn't think twice to ask the price of some groovy new cocktail. The alliance of bar and restaurant also explains why we are flocking to gastropubs, happily having a g'n't at the bar whilst looking at the wine list, as we wait for our dinner to be ready.

THE RESTAURANT WITH ROOMS

Country restaurants need rooms for people to overnight in when they come for dinner. City dwellers can take taxis and public transport home, but down the country people will no longer take a drink and then drive themselves home: the risk is too great.

But, aside from the risk, we need to approach this question by focusing on the idyll a restaurant is offering. Dinner out should be an event, but if someone cannot have a glass of wine with their food, it is much less of an event. Yet, the hard-working person having dinner on a Friday evening really wants that drink.

It's been a long week and they want to chill.

So, what to do? The answer is to offer rooms. Ideally, the rooms should be simple and inexpensive. Why? In order that their economic impact on the overall cost of the evening is not too great, and in order that their economic impact on your start-up costs can be controlled down to the tightest cent.

And simple rooms also leave the focus of the visit on dinner, which is what you, as a restaurateur, are aiming to achieve.

And simple rooms also let people concentrate on each other, which is what the restaurant with rooms is all about: cash-rich, time-poor, and lacking quality time together, there are innumerable couples who desperately want that idyll to last just as long as possible.

The value element of all this is crucial in delivering relaxed customers. So, if your guests think the rooms are good value, and they don't have to drive which means they will drink an extra bottle of wine, and if they can also lie in bed in the morning and get some quality time, then you have the ideal customer: an extremely grateful one.

You have extended their idyll beyond a good dinner into a complete chill-out experience with quality time between two busy people who don't have half-enough time to talk to one another. And they don't need a grand room: remember, your focus is cooking and that is the attraction: the room is the add on that makes the experience of enjoying the cooking all the better. And don't forget that it is a restaurant, with rooms. Not an hotel. Not a country house. A RwR.

So, if they want a lift to their room, and someone to carry their bags, and room service, then they are in the wrong place. Never lose the all-important focus on the food.

primer

• Value is not the same thing as cost. It is a more complex concept, and one that is vital to success.

• Value for money will create regular customers, and regular customers are the easiest customers to deal with.

• Price your food and drinks in such a way that each element offers value, from the cup of coffee to the house champagne.

• Make money slowly, because if customers feel that you are out to wring every last cent out of them, they don't like it.

• Make a reputation first, and your reputation will make money for you for decades.

• Consider all the elements of your restaurant, and consider whether they can be sold to the customer: extend the offer beyond food and wine.

• Beautiful bars make money, allow customers to relax whilst not feeling that they are waiting, and allow you to orchestrate your dining room.

• Country restaurants need rooms in which people can overnight. This makes the customers more relaxed, and increases their spend.

Ben Gorman, The Mermaid Café, Dublin

• Learn to cook. Nice dinner parties don't count.

• It's harder to be a waiter than a chef. Waiters have to be nice to nasty people.

• Really good chefs are nice to waiters.

• Staff breakfast and tea are the most important part of the day. They must happen on time, altogether, before service.

• Staff meals cause the most rows. Tips next, then rotas.

• Health and safety officers have to be Nazis. There are too many idiots in this business.

• Mice get through holes smaller than a Biro's diameter.

• We had two chefs dating for $2^1/_2$ years without anyone knowing. Pure professionalism.
Never employ couples, frown on inter-staff relationships. Marriage guidance, drugs counselling, nursing, agony aunt are all important skills of the restaurateur.

• Highly expensive concentrated detergents always get used undiluted.

• Drinking a bottle of wine is the easiest way to wind down after service. Not the healthiest.

"THE QUALITIES OF AN EXCEPTIONAL COOK ARE AKIN TO THOSE OF A SUCCESSFUL TIGHTROPE WALKER: AN ABIDING PASSION FOR THE TASK, COURAGE TO GO OUT ON A LIMB, AND AN IMPECCABLE SENSE OF BALANCE."

BRYAN MILLER

9

9

"The Proust madeleine phenomenon is now as firmly established in folklore as Newton's apple or Watt's steam kettle. The man ate a tea biscuit, the taste evoked memories, he wrote a book. This is capable of expression by the formula TMB, for Taste=Memory=Book."

A.J. LIEBLING

THE COOKERY BOOKS TO HAVE ON TOP OF THE FRIDGE

One of the tasks I set myself in the course of any consultancy project is to compile a reading list of books on food, cookery and wine that will be appropriate to the project.

The business of cooking, after all, requires the chef to be familiar with contemporary styles, whilst at the same time having a sure footing in knowing where historical dishes have arisen from, and how they have been adapted over the years.

Cookery books are also provocative: they set the mind buzzing with new flavour ideas and combinations, or they reanimate older ideas thanks to placing them in a new context. At best, they can do both, demonstrating a contemporary twist on a classic culinary concept. Hell, at best they can change your life: just ask American cooks about Richard Olney.

The best cooks use cookery books as an extra ingredient, endlessly learning from their favourite texts, and hungrily seeking new ideas from newly published works.

This process of the project ought to be simple, but it has sometimes led to a clash with chefs. For instance, I want them to see and analyse the smart, down-to-earth, well-measured cooking ideas from Danny Meyer in *The Union Square Café Cookbook*, so that they might understand how Meyer became the most significant figure in recent New York culinary history, by the simple expedient of cooking the sort of food that people like to eat.

Or I might want them to wonder at the elegant simplicity of the food that made Bill Granger the hottest restaurateur in Sydney; food ideas from breakfast to dinner that are irresistible.

They, however, want to make some phantasmagorical construction out of a Charlie Trotter book – they would really,

really love to make that pudding that features Chateau d'Yquem in the sauce – or else they want to play some little fun game with Thomas Keller's glam *The French Laundry Cookbook*. They would just love to cook Keller's jokey "Fish and Chips" – red mullet with a palette d'ail doux and garlic chips.

Well, wrap that up in newspaper for me.

If they bring in a copy of Marco Pierre White's *White Heat*, then I know there is some painful frustration lying ahead in my work. *White Heat* signals that they don't really want to be chefs: they want to be Napoleon, and they want Bob Carlos Clarke to take their picture.

Cookery books by chefs, with some distinguished exceptions, are largely useless, albeit that they do contain some eye-catching eye candy in the form of glamorous and unrealistic photography.

Chef's books are unhelpful because they conform to the old competitive, hierarchical shibboleth that does such damage to good cooking, and which feeds so many male egos that scarcely need any further engorgement: Look at me! they holler. Look at all my expensive ingredients! Look at how fussy my food is! Adore me!

Smart cookery books, on the other hand, books that explore the culture of cookery, do not beg to be adored, and at their best they manage the supremely difficult task of creating something delicious, and explaining exactly why it works. Chief amongst these, in my opinion, is Denis Cotter's *The Café Paradiso Cookbook*, because, more than any other book, here is a text that lets us know how a chef thinks and works. Cotter takes us inside his creativity, a task chefs are either unable or, in many cases, unwilling to do.

THE WELL-READ RESTAURATEUR
petits • propos • culinaires

Cotter is able to place his cooking within the greater picture of the working restaurant. "Bread wakes up our kitchen early in the morning, and comes to life as the kitchen does, finally emerging from the oven when the place has become a flurry of activity, smells, noise and a slight nervousness about the impending lunch. I can't imagine working in a restaurant kitchen that didn't make its own bread."

Believe it or not, but that glorious piece of writing is the first recipe paragraph in this extraordinary book, and in it Denis Cotter sets out two stalls: the intellectual ability of a chef to see cooking in the abstract and artistic sense – "bread wakes up our kitchen" – whilst establishing his culinary credentials with impeccable forcefulness – "I can't imagine working in a restaurant kitchen that didn't make its own bread."

150 pages later, and Cotter signs off, leaving you reeling at the end of an extraordinary culinary journey, mesmerised by the sophistication and earthiness of the ideas promulgated and provocated in this book.

What makes *The Café Paradiso Cookbook* all the more remarkable, of course, is that this is a cookery book that has no recipes using meat, game or fowl. This is cooking with vegetables, grains, pulses, cheeses, herbs and so on, what we might, in an old-fashioned way, call "vegetarian" cooking.

What it is, of course, is simply creative, original and challenging cooking, the sort of thing every cook worth his pinch of salt should aim to achieve with every service.

I deal with *The Café Paradiso Cookbook* book at greater detail elsewhere in this book, but I would regard it as the cookery ur-text for contemporary cooks. No less impressive, and no less essential, is Mr Cotter's second book, *Paradiso Seasons*.

Finding the right books to spur imaginations and to help focus the content of the menu demands different texts for different destinations. Here, for instance, is a list I suggested for a coffee shop that had a busy lunchtime trade:

The Café Paradiso Cookbook, Denis Cotter (Atrium)

Marie Claire Flavours, Donna Hay (Murdoch Books)

Real Food, Nigel Slater (4th Estate)

The Greens Cookbook, Deborah Madison (Bantam)

Vegetarian Cooking for Everyone, Deborah Madison (Broadway Books)

The Silver Palate Cookbooks, Julee Rosso & Shiela Lukins (Workman)

The Dean & DeLuca Cookbook (Ebury Press)

The 125 Best Recipes Ever, Loyd Grossman (Michael Joseph)

Roast Chicken & Other Stories, Simon Hopkinson (Ebury)

Hot Food, Paul & Jeanne Rankin (Mitchell Beazley)

Nantucket Open House Cookbook, Sarah Leah Chase (Workman)

Pizza Defined, Bernadette O'Shea (Estragon Press)

The Cook's Companion, Stephanie Alexander (Viking)

The Union Square Café Cookbook, Meyer & Romano (Harper Collins)

This list was designed to take the users away from the world of television-themed books they had been using, and into fine professional works that are imaginative, reliable and creative.

Any cook will learn a huge amount from Simon Hopkinson's book, or from Loyd Grossman's meticulously chosen century and more of dishes. Deborah Madison's books, both from her work in San Francisco's Greens Restaurant and her later, enormous studies, are fertile ground for the apt pupil. The books by Sarah Leah Chase and Paul and Jeanne Rankin are suffused with the intelligence and wit of smart cooks, and Ms Chase was also one of the key movers behind the original Silver Palate books, which collated the work of New York's famous deli. The deli theme occurs again in the huge and hugely impressive *Dean & De Luca Cookbook*, a treasure trove of smart ideas.

Nigel Slater, Donna Hay, Bernadette O'Shea and Stephanie Alexander are individual, quirky cooks, cooks whose work has the ability to make you look again and again at simple ideas.

But aside from the many choices that one can make from contemporary cookery books, there is another potential list, of cookery books by writers that are outstanding works of art in their own right, books that can stand as a companion to any and every cook, thanks to their ability to inspire, and to explain and evoke the entire culture of cookery.

• **Richard Olney,** *Simple French Food*

SFF is perhaps the most elegant and elegiac book ever written on cooking. But it's elegiac tone is underpinned by the astounding culinary imagination of Olney, the man who oversaw all 27 volumes of the Time-Life *The Good Cook* series. In his introduction, Olney writes of how "I would like my readers to share with me the belief that food and wine must be an essential part of the whole life, in which the sensuous-sensual-spiritual elements are so intimately interwoven that the incomplete exploitation of any one can only result in imperfection". There, in one sentence, is every reason why we want to cook.

• **Patience Gray,** *Honey from a Weed*

Richard Olney summons up a sense of place – Provence – but Patience Gray – who once wrote a conventional, witty little cookery book in the 1950's called *Plats du Jour* – evokes not only place but also time in this incredible book, which reads as if the author is in a dream. There are recipes, but they aren't the point.

• Elizabeth David, *French Provincial Cooking*

This is the masterpiece from a distinguished body of work by one of the great culinary explorers. Mrs David has become decidedly unfashionable since her death, but her writings, and in particular her journalism, are thoughtful and creative, and she, more than anyone, helped construct the appreciative mentality for food and cooking that we all take for granted today.

• Marcella Hazan, *Marcella Cucina*

Any of Marcella Hazan's books reveal not only her intuitive and studied grasp of why Italian cooking works, but also the razor-sharp mind of Victor Hazan, who was responsible for a lot of the text. In *Marcella Cucina*, it is Marcella alone, and if the book is less scholarly, it is no less inspirational.

• Jane Grigson, *Good Things*

A good cook will own all of Mrs Grigson's books, for they are a template of considered, scholarly food writing. But *Good Things* is a beauty: "This is not a manual of cookery, but a book about enjoying food" is how she opens the text, and it's bliss all the way to the end.

• Claudia Roden, *A Book of Middle Eastern Food*

Few cookery books are truly inexhaustible, but this great classic does seem to be a bottomless fount of marvellous ideas, and not merely inexhaustible, but also timeless.

• Alice Waters, Chez Panisse Vegetables

It is invidious to pick any one of Alice Water's eight Panisse books – and that includes her children's cookery book, *Fanny at Chez Panisse* – but the blend of scholarly enquiry and instinctive culinary creativity in the Vegetables volume may just be Panisse's finest work.

• MFK Fisher, *The Art of Eating*

A collection of five of Mary Frances Kennedy Fisher's books, which are not really books about cooking, but books that are about MFK Fisher and cooking, and eating, and drinking. No other food writer can match the wit of this prose: MFK is the Comden and Green of food writing.

• Julie Sahni, *Classic Indian Cooking*

I love this book, and can't understand why it doesn't occupy pole position amongst ethnic cookery books, a field where texts are frequently compromised for Western tastes. Ms Sahni's book is glorious.

"WITH FOOD, IT'S NOT WHAT YOU DO TO IT, IT'S BEST WHAT YOU DON'T DO TO IT. YOU MUST RESPECT THE FLAVOUR AND TEXTURE. IF YOU TAKE A DUCK LEG, AND YOU LOOK AT IT, MOTHER NATURE TELLS YOU WHERE TO CUT. YOU TAKE THAT TO EVERYTHING YOU TOUCH."

DAVID GUMBLETON

primer

• **Great cookery books are a vital source of information and inspiration to any kitchen.**

• **Be sparing in cooking from the books of well-known contemporary chefs: if you are doing it, chances are scores of others are doing it too.**

• **The most valuable cookery books explore and explain the entire culture of food and cooking.**

• **Explore older cookery books, and don't limit yourself simply to contemporary titles.**

• **Cook theme dinners from your favourite cookery books.**

• **Don't be afraid to use recipes in a book as a springboard for your own improvisation.**

• **Cookery books make for smart decoration.**

• **Have the ambition to write your own book.**

10

10

"A critic is a bundle of biases held loosely together by a sense of taste."

WHITNEY BALLIETT

MANAGING THE MEDIA

Of the many things about the restaurant business that continue to surprise me, perhaps the most startling and perennial factor is the belief of many restaurateurs that they do not need to deal with the media.

For every restaurateur who opens up shop and sends an e-mail or an envelope stuffed with menus, wine list, fliers, details and whatnot, and who tentatively suggests that the writer-critic-publisher-producer might like to visit at a time convenient to them, there are a dozen places who simply don't bother.

Even worse, believe it or not, are those incipient restaurateurs who will call on the telephone, and tell you that they have just opened. Fine, you reply, can you post me menus, wine list and details.

And they never do. Never. What is it with restaurateurs and the postal service?

Every year, after we have finished compiling our annual Bridgestone Guides, I will inevitably happen upon a place a week or so later that would have merited inclusion in the guide, had I only known about its existence and managed to have it inspected before the book was published.

The restaurant could have garnered publicity and increased their visibility and viability, had they simply bothered to mail out to the media the fact that they had opened for business.

You cannot afford to pass up on the free – and incredibly valuable – publicity offered to restaurants by the media. It is via the media that your restaurant will become known to everyone other than locals.

So, right from the outset, you need to have a media strategy: you need to Manage the Media.

Simon Pratt, Leylie Hayes, Teresa Byrne, Avoca Handweavers, Wicklow & Dublin

1. DON'T BE UNDER CAPITALISED STARTING OFF

The difference between a roaring success and abject and costly failure is 15%. If things go great you could make 7.5% If they don't you will lose 7.5%.

It is very difficult to be on the right side of this fulcrum from the start. Everything has to appear to be right to the customer and critic starting off. You need to make sure it is, and therefore tweaking the equation to make money will have to come afterwards. You need to allow for this in your early projections.

2. INVEST IN THE RIGHT STAFF AND KEEP INVESTING IN THEM

The right people make all the difference; in fact one good person is worth two or more passengers. It is hard to always remember and to make time but do appreciate your staff and keep training and encouraging them.

3. CONSISTENCY IS VITAL

You have to do it right and keep doing it right.

4. QUALITY IN QUALITY OUT

Be sure to source the best produce all the time. With the wrong ingredients it will always be an uphill struggle.

5. COST OF STAFF

The most difficult number to get right in Ireland today is the staffing/labour cost. You are essentially starting a manufacturing business in a first world economy when all other manufacturing based industries are moving to a lower cost country. You can't, of course, move to a cheaper cost base. The following need to be addressed:

• A smaller number of good staff that are well rewarded.

• A well-designed restaurant is much more efficient.

• A manageable length menu.

6. HYGIENE, CLEANLINESS AND HACCP COMPLIANCE ARE VITAL

7. YOU NEED TO BE BUSY

Everything can fall into place if a restaurant

is busy at least five out of seven days. Can your proposed location/chosen style of cuisine deliver this?

- Think fresh produce
- Think overheads
- Think staffing cost

8. COSTS OF INGREDIENTS AND ANCILLARY PRODUCTS

Make time to check prices with your suppliers and in the market place.

9. GET EXPERIENCE

Try to work in successful restaurants and hire staff with good experience. Its harder and more costly to learn on your own (we should know!).

10. GIVE THE CUSTOMERS WHAT THEY WANT

Currently an easy, accessible, affordable and relaxed style of restaurant is what the market wants. Good food and service in a welcoming environment.

Easy really.

MEDIA MANAGEMENT

If you are opening a high-profile place in a city and have a posse of investors behind you, the chances are that you will want to secure every inch of media attention you can get, and that you will have enough money to pay for it.

If you want this, hire a public relations firm, but not any old firm: hire someone who specialises in food, restaurants and the hospitality industry. If you don't choose carefully, then you will wind up paying someone who will have sent out an enormous and enormously expensive mailshot... to all the wrong people. Those people will have removed your glossy brochure from its envelope, and put it straight in the bin.

But there is a second difficulty with hiring a PR firm. They will work on the launch of the restaurant, unless you place them on an expensive retainer to continue the hunt for media coverage. But, frequently, it is only three or four months down the line that the really important and significant opportunities for valuable media coverage emerge. How do you make sure you don't miss them?

The answer is to regard managing the media as an on-going part of the whole business of running a restaurant. And the best way to practice this is to have a media management operator in-house. Doing media management in-house also allows the office to manage information distributed on a regular basis to your customers, a vital part of maintaining your customer base. But, let's look at the media first.

THE MEDIA

Maybe those new restaurants who don't communicate their details to the media presume that they would be disturbing people who are already very busy.

If they believe that, then they need to realise a simple fact about the media and how it works: every writer needs a story and, when that story has been processed and eaten up, the writer needs another new story. The media is voracious, so feed it.

And the time to feed it is when their diet of information is at its most meagre: offering a good story in the third week of January is good, but expecting a writer to get back to you when the Christmas rush is on in early December is not only naïve, it is plain crazy. Timing is everything. Timing and targeting.

The targeting of information is vital. You do it by buying all the newspapers and magazines which might be read by your potential audience, scanning through them and finding out which writers might be receptive to receiving your information. You don't write to features editors, far less to "The Editor": you hunt out the person whose job involves passing on the sort of information you have.

You do the same thing with visual media, and also with the electronic media. In every newspaper, magazine, television programme or on-line media, there is someone who will welcome the details of your new opening, new winter menu, new additions to the wine list, new charity dinner, whatever. If you get to the right person, then they run the story, your potential audience read it, then pick up the telephone and make a booking. None of this costs you any money.

And, after you have the daily media sorted, then you do the same with guidebooks. Buy them all, then target them all. And not just the food-related guides: you want to be in the Where to Eat sections of the general guidebooks as well.

And you do this on an on-going basis, across a broad spectrum of media. You supply recipes to cookery magazines. You supply details of special offers to news media. You write to travel editors to tell them that the next time they are commissioning a piece about Dublin/West Cork/Connemara, wherever, then you would be delighted to help. You send new menus to the editors of culinary guides and you keep them up to date with any changes that have happened. You supply details of what you are doing to on-line event guides. Wherever there is media, there is the potential for coverage. And not just when you open, but every week, every month, every year. A restaurant creates a narrative, and the narrative never stops.

The one way in which you can spoil this, however, is by adopting the wrong tone. The media are not under an obligation to give you free publicity, so if you annoy them by adopting a presumptuous or demanding tone, then you will make an enemy who will be determined to never give you any coverage.

So, the way in which you get it right is to presume nothing, and to simply see your job as the distribution of information on a regular basis to selected targets who have an interest in conveying your information to their readers and viewers. And your information should be sent in the form of a letter: hello, enjoy your work, hope the following might be of interest, if I can be of any help then please get back to me, maybe we will see you down here some time, all the best, yours sincerely...

First time out, you may get little or no response. Don't be deterred: it could be your timing was bad, so try again. Restaurants always have a story to tell, so tell it, and keep telling it.

If you are lucky, and you are a charismatic person, then you will wind up having to keep the media at bay: just look at the massive media coverage restaurateurs such as Terence Conran or Ken Buggy or Oliver Peyton or Derry Clarke receive for whatever new venture they are embarking upon. Cultivate the right targets in the media, and you will be facing the same – pleasurable – problem.

And, of course, managing the media all by yourself saves any costs that you might be considering spending on advertising. Editorial not only gets your message across more accurately, it also gets it across in a more prestigious manner.

MANAGING THE MEDIA
listen • for • silence

But managing your information has another vital – and possibly more important – target audience: your customers.

I am always astonished that restaurants do not use the internet to relay to their regular customers the details of whatever new changes, events and happenings are taking place in the restaurant.

If you build a database of your customers e-mail addresses, then at the touch of a single button you can have your information distributed for virtually nothing to the target audience that matters most.

Working on the assumption that 80% of your business will come from 20% of your customers – a standard rule in retailing – then you must ensure that those 20% are the first to receive details of what you are doing. You want to make that 20% feel special, you want to make them feel like insiders, so get their e-mail addresses and – briefly, occasionally – keep them up to date with what you are doing. This subtle provocation cements the relationship between customer and restaurateur, and keeps you at the forefront of their mind. Remember, you are in competition for their patronage, so look after them.

THE CRITICS

Restaurateurs are obsessed with critics, and critical rating. Whilst I was preparing this book, a media firestorm broke out over the apparent suicide of French chef Bernard Loiseau, which was allegedly provoked by his restaurant being knocked down a few points by the *Gault-Millau Guide*.

Everywhere you look, the rating of restaurants is always hierarchical: 4 stars from the *New York Times*, so many points out of 20 in *The Guardian*, wines lists that are stuffed with irrelevant details such as how many points out of 100 the wine writer Robert Parker has decided a particular wine is worthy of; what is your rating in *Zagat* or *Harden's* or, whilst we are at it, are you an Icon or are you a Classic in *The Bridgestone Guides*?

This competitive culture does restaurants serious harm, because it stresses competition – a hierarchy – over the value of individuality; it rewards compliance with a critical scheme in preference to taking the time to describe a signature style.

Trying to turn away from this, trying to make the system more abstract and individual, as we have tried to do in our Bridgestone Guides, often causes incomprehension amongst readers. I mean, if Michelin give you 2 stars but you don't feature in the Bridgestones, then what on earth is going on? If the critics can't agree, how on earth can the punters know where to go?

It is my belief that this hierarchical system is being slowly undermined, and what is undermining it is a confident, experienced public; people who know their own minds.

And what further undermines the system is the frequently atrocious standards of criticism tolerated by newspaper and magazine editors. No one artistic group suffers so much from the ignorance of fools as the restaurant business.

Music critics – with the exception of people who write about popular music – know their stuff. Architecture critics and art critics and literary critics are schooled and trained and passionate.

But restaurant writers are frequently little more than megalomaniacs with a passionate regard for their own opinions. What you get, all too often, is opinion, and opinion is not criticism. In fact, it is the antithesis of criticism.

So, where do you get accurate, balanced criticism from, if not the media?

The answer is: you get it from your customers. If you are attracting and continually satisfying customers, then you are doing the job properly. If repeat business is slow, then you are not doing the job right.

Consider these two rather different approaches to criticism: the first from Hong Kong, the second from Kenmare, Co Kerry.

LISTEN FOR THE SILENCE

Hong Kong food critics do not deliver stinging verdicts in print. Instead, their method is to ignore the places they do not favour, which means that the restaurateur must listen for The Silence.

You don't need to have Hong Kong reviewers failing to chat about you to realise that listening for the silence is a smart way to gauge the success of what you are doing.

Irish people are effusive, for the most part: if something is good, they will tell you that it is good, so long as you give them the opportunity, and that does not mean leaning over the table, as they are in mid-meal and mid-conversation, and asking "Is everything alright?".

What it means is frankly canvassing them at the right moment, and asking if they were genuinely happy with the food and the service and the experience, and if they weren't then you would appreciate being told so that you can do something about it.

Doing it this way is completely different to the traditional mid-meal enquiry, which will elicit nothing. You have to get a genuine sense of feedback from your customers, and if you are listening to them, and all you are getting back is The Silence, then something is wrong.

Certain restaurants manage this process extremely well; usually those places where a proprietor can work the room, meeting and greeting and, above all, listening. Are you getting genuine feedback which is positive about what you are doing? Or are you being brushed off with "Fine, thank you", or "Very nice, thank you".

When you hear those words, those weasel words of customers who don't want to tell you right out that they are not happy, then you are hearing The Silence and, chances are, you won't see those customers again.

You don't have to get out of them precisely what they are not happy about – though if you can manage to do that at the right time (help them on with their coats, that's the best time), then so much the better. You simply have to realise that something is missing if, in an interactive entertainment like a restaurant, you are not getting the equivalent of a round of applause at the end of the performance. Then you are in trouble. The trouble may not be immediate, but you are going to run into it soon.

And it's not enough to aim just for a round of applause; you want an encore, you want those customers back. A movie or a show that gets no applause is doomed: a restaurant that is hearing The Silence is, likewise, on the road to nowhere.

ONE BAD MEAL LOSES 100 CUSTOMERS

It was that inspired restaurateur, Maura Foley of Kenmare, County Kerry, who postulated this controversial thought in her testimony in the first edition of this book.

Initially, I thought the figure was, surely, an exaggeration. But, as I began to ask people in the business what they thought about the remark, a general consensus emerged that Mrs Foley was not merely not exaggerating, but that her figure of 100 lost customers could even be on the conservative side.

Can it be true? One bad experience means that 100 punters will not darken your door? I reckon it is, but I think there is slightly more to the remark than first appears.

If something goes wrong for a customer and you don't handle it or you handle it badly, then, yes, 100 customers will have you marked down as a dead zone within 2 or 3 days of the incident.

People love to talk about food, and what they talk about even more than good experiences is the bad experiences: for every e-mail we receive at the Bridgestone Guides from a food lover telling us about a hot new address, we will receive 15 telling us about people who got it wrong and handled it badly.

People say the Irish don't complain? Don't believe it for a second. They complain in the most effective, most efficient, way: they tell all their friends that you are rubbish, they write to guide books to tell us that you are rubbish, and they will keep on telling everyone who will listen that you are rubbish until the next bad experience comes along. Give them six months, and it will be 200-300 punters who won't be queueing up to walk through your doors.

What to do? As the chef and writer Paul Flynn points out in his testimony in this book, you simply must not let a customer with a genuine grievance leave the restaurant with their grievance intact.

"The customer must always leave the restaurant satisfied" warns Mr Flynn. It really is that simple.

This does not mean placating the impossible customer, that person whom you should take great pleasure in evicting from your restaurant at the earliest moment. It means taking care of the person with a genuine grievance, and turning that grievance into an acceptance that in a human business things must go wrong, turning it into an acceptance of human frailty, a frailty which, if you handle the situation right, will have them understandingly accepting of what went wrong, rather than simply being furious about it.

So, this is the sort of criticism, from the sort of critic you really have to pay attention to, that you must cure, correct, and vow will never happen again. Of course it will happen again, then you must cure and correct one more time.

TESTIMONY

Susan Holland & Ian Parr, The Customs House, Baltimore, County Cork

1. Work ethic	6. Clientele (thanks everyone)
2. Ingredients	7. Ambience (it's only food)
3. Interest in food	8. Bank manager
4. Experience	9. Cultural baggage
5. Location	10. Sense of humour

primer

• Manage relationships with the media in-house in order to achieve successful exposure.

• Media management is not a once-off thing; you have to do it all the time, continuously feeding information to newspapers, magazines and electronic media.

• Create a database of your customers' details and use this to send them up-to-the-minute information about new developments in the restaurant, via the internet.

• Don't be fixated on the critics in the media: it is the critics sitting eating in your restaurant - your customers - who you should be fixated on.

• If all you are hearing from your customers is silence, then something is seriously wrong.

• One bad meal will lose you 100 customers, and possibly many more.

Harry McKeogh, Cherry Tree Restaurant, Killaloe, County Clare

1. CATCHMENT AREA

Identifying the catchment area in which to locate your restaurant, taking into consideration accessibility and the parking space available.

2. DISPOSABLE INCOMES

Disposable incomes within that area - corporate, tourism and local business.

3. EXPERIENCE AND REPUTATION

Your own experience and reputation within the restaurant industry.

4. SYSTEMS

Experience in all areas of running a restaurant from kitchen porter to head chef, waiting to restaurant management, so as to be confident to set your own systems and high standards.

5. MAINTENANCE

Knowledge of accounts, marketing, building maintenance, plumbing, electrics, preventative maintenance system in place.

6. STANDARDS

Consistent high standard of food and service using the best quality local produce available.

7. FLAIR FOR FOOD AND LOVE OF WINE

Flair for food and love of wine, enjoyment of entertaining in aesthetic surroundings providing a sense of occasion for every customer when they come to dine.

8. IN-HOUSE TRAINING

Experienced staff in key positions, friendly, good humoured, with in-house training on-going for all staff.

9. COMMUNICATION SKILLS

Good communication skills in dealing with customer enquiries, reservations and orders.

10. CLEANLINESS AND PERSONAL HYGIENE

High standard of restaurant cleanliness and personal hygiene of staff.

11

11

"I put two lessons from
The Cocky Cactus at the top of my list:
a restaurant can be fairly humble
and still feel world-class, and nothing
will build loyalty like 'loving'
relationships with customers."

JEREMIAH TOWER

JEREMIAH TOWER

MAKING REVOLUTION

Jeremiah Tower's autobiography, *California Dish: What I saw (and cooked) at the American Culinary Revolution* is deeply fascinating, and deeply flawed.

The flawed bits are not simply the book's lop-sided structure, but lie mainly with Tower's relentless carping about the very many people he worked and dealt with during his career as one of America's most successful and high-profile chefs and restaurateurs.

From Chez Panisse through the Santa Fe Bar & Grill and onto his triumph with San Francisco's Stars restaurant, Tower made enemies and he uses his book to tell us what he thinks of them now and how they behaved then. Discretion, Jeremiah obviously reckoned, is not the better part of valour.

In particular, Tower has a major problem with the fact that Alice Waters, of Berkeley's Chez Panisse restaurant, is a world-famous restaurant personality and food guru, whilst Tower reckons that it was actually his cooking, when he was a partner at Panisse in the mid-1970's, that actually made the restaurant celebrated for the first time. The fact that Tower is himself particularly well-known and much respected for his modern American cooking doesn't seem to allow him to forgive Alice for being such a superstar.

But the fascinating bits are worth the price of the ticket, in particular the education of this particular aesthete, and his journey into and through gastronomy, a journey which echoes the lives of other American food aesthetes such as M.F.K. Fisher and Richard Olney.

Along with this fascinating history, Tower does two other things brilliantly: he writes about the clamour and mayhem of being a restaurateur, and in particular about a typical day at Stars, with an energy and chutzpah that is intoxicating – I really hope Baz Luhrman buys the rights and makes a movie about this day in the life – for this is a roller-coaster ride powered by champagne and cocaine and egotism.

"I wanted people to feel they owned my restaurant, as if it had everything for them rather than something for everyone," he writes.

"I had visions of a place full of lawyers and city politicians selling us all down the river at lunch, afternoons at the bar full of glad victories or unhappy defeats from the law courts next door, the cocktail hour with all the office workers in the area, the pre-theater crowd, a full house for dinner, and then post-10:00pm the restaurant full again with the stars of the performing arts eating oysters and drinking champagne, with fans coming by to ogle the lithe young bodies of the corps de ballet. Filling the place four to five times a day was the dream."

My kind of restaurant.

Secondly, he writes about the importance of restaurant menus, and the utilisation of menus as a signal of reviving a country's gastronomic heritage and powering that heritage forward. It is quite shocking, at a time when American chefs such as Tower, Waters and those who have come after them have been so successful in forging a relationship between great restaurants and artisan suppliers, to be reminded of a time in American restaurants when most of the stuff came out of a can or a packet.

It is in this area that Tower shows how a clever, determined chef, and especially one with a brilliant eye for publicity, can create nothing less than a revolution in restaurant practices, a revolution that can have a powerful impact on a country's food culture. Back in 1976, Tower was being influenced by writers such as James Villas calling for "the possible existence in the United States of a slowly developing formalized American cuisine, a stylized native cookery that might one day rival the European and Far Eastern culinary traditions."

Later in the book, Tower can write that this very question had been answered by the end of the century, when "the entire revolution reached its full fruition." The key element was "a vision that allowed a new simplicity to be recognised and welcomed as being as important as the temples of red-plush French, old Italian and Continental American food and restaurants beloved by previous generations."

In other words, make it new, and make it your own. Tower recognises that out of every chef's individual menus must arise a national menu, a menu that is political, social and cultural, a menu that accords the necessary respect to the two most important artisans of all: cooks and farmers.

It is the duty of every new generation of chefs to overthrow the old guard, and to re-state the principles upon which great cooking can take place: seasonality; locality; creativity. The great Australian food writer, Leo Schofield, writing about Tower's Stars restaurant, wrote that he felt he was "witnessing the death of the old culture as defined as an evening spent out with a three-course meal".

I have no doubt that the chefs in Sydney and Melbourne would say the same, and believe the same, just as the chefs in Spain, right now, are dancing to the beat of a different drum, a drum that has no time for the classical French cooking and service that intellectually and practically dominated the 20th century.

"Any winning restaurateur these days realizes that outstanding cooking starts with superb ingredients, and that a menu should be conceived from the marketplace rather than abstractly thought up," writes Tower, again summarising the inherent political radicalism of this act via the writing of a menu.

Towards the end of the book, he writes of how a 1990 "Tasting of Summer Produce" in Berkeley "made everyone realize what a powerful union the three main players made: supplier, chef and restaurant customer could change completely the culinary scene of a locality in just twenty years."

This is fighting talk, particularly for European sensibilities reared on "tradition", but the experience of chefs in Australia and America over the last three decades show that it can be done, that it has been done. And the stagnation of creative cooking in France in recent years shows what happens if you stop wishing to make revolution.

But it has to begin somewhere, and for Tower it can be summed up as "a sensual love for the flavor and texture of beautiful ingredients. And knowing how to marry them."

That is the theme throughout this culinary life's journey, and I think it is worth stressing that without that "sensual love" for food and cooking, one has little chance of being a great or important cook or restaurateur. Tower is intoxicated by the ability of this love of food and cooking, in disparate individuals, to lead to the need to create great restaurants, to foment the hunger to create the greatest entertainments of our lives.

JEREMIAH TOWER
supplier • chef • customer

"EACH TIME YOU CLIMB IN THE BUSINESS YOU GET MORE PRESSURE, AND THE MORE YOU CLIMB THE BETTER ABLE YOU ARE TO COPE WITH THAT PRESSURE, AND WE NEED THAT PRESSURE, IT'S WHAT COOKING NEEDS"

KEVIN THORNTON

primer

• Menus should have two ambitions. Firstly, to state your own preferences and personality. Secondly, they should aim to be a part of a national menu.

• Great food cultures can be created in a short period of time. Supplier, chef and customer, pulling together, can make it happen.

• Every new generation must overthrow the old guard.

Caroline Workman, food writer, consultant, foodstuffireland.com

1. Don't think about opening up a restaurant until you've experienced and enjoyed a full-time, medium-term, responsible job in the trade.

2. You must love dealing with all members of the general public - not just the people you like.

3. The more successful you are, the harder you should work to make sure the people you have to turn away will come back. There will always be leaner times.

4. Don't tell staff about new projects or improvements you wish to make unless you are sure you can deliver them quickly.

5. Lead by example and be hands-on but do not be afraid to delegate, so that you have time to think beyond day-to-day business. Delegate the nice jobs too.

6. Never be complacent: your business can always be better.

7. Most staff members will thrive on additional responsibility and a sense of sharing your business. Make sure they are suitably challenged.

8. Encourage staff members to think on your behalf and make sure you implement their good ideas.

9. Your waiters and waitresses are your sales reps and your market researchers. Choose them well, train them well, pay them well and learn about your customers from them.

10. Make sure staff members have tasted everything you serve and that they can describe food and wine with enthusiasm and confidence.

11. Stamp out any signs of an "us and them" culture between the kitchen and the front of house team, or between staff and management. Customers will sense any friction.

12. Take delight in a busy restaurant, rather than treating it as hard work.

13. Share only good news with your customers, and in apology situations, just let them know the solution.
Do not be tempted to tell them about any difficulties.

14. Pro-actively cultivate good relationships with people and businesses in your neighbourhood and contribute to community events.

12

12

"Places, as well as tastes, are locked up in food. The clear perfumed stillness of a bottle of flower water, the sexy, velvety skin on a fig, the sunburnt blood colour of a jar of cayenne. Our love of foods has as much to do with what they represent as with what they taste like."

DIANA HENRY

THE WELL-TRAVELLED RESTAURATEUR

One of the most important things any restaurateur needs, in order to survive and prosper, is an airline ticket that takes you away from your restaurant, and then brings you back again, suffused with new ideas and inspirations that you have learnt on your travels. Good cooks and restaurateurs must travel in order to learn.

Such culinary journeys are vital in keeping yourself abreast of just what is going on out there, because the international world of cooking is seismic, and explosions of interest keep erupting in unlikely places.

After all, who would have believed that Australia, a country not so long ago associated with Foster's lager and *pie-an'* (meat pie and tomato ketchup) could have shoved itself to the forefront of global cooking, thanks to chefs such as Neil Perry, Tetsuya Wakuda and Bill Granger, to name merely a trio of great chefs and restaurateurs.

Australia is proof that any country can seize the culinary initiative and build that national menu based on exploiting local foods, so long as they don't remain hidebound to the past. As Bill Granger has said, analysing the informal and rule-free approach that took Australian cooking to the forefont, "We don't do formality well. When we try to do formal fashion, it's a dog. When we do beachwear, surfwear, jeans, it's fantastic."

Australian cooking slipped in under the net, proof that the only rules that matter are whatever ones you want to play by. And it has been fascinating, during the 1990's, to see French cooking lose its pre-eminence amongst global opinion, as French chefs have argued – bitterly – about the way forward. Tradition or innovation? they ask, which is a truly dumb question. If cookery and restaurants do not innovate, they die. The Californians, the New Yorkers, the folk in Sydney and Melbourne, San Sebastian and Madrid and Barcelona have all left the French at the starting blocks, simply because innovation has driven their respective food and restaurant cultures.

But let's not be too hard on the beleaguered French, for any chef and restaurateur who came of age during the last 25 years would have owed an enormous debt to that posse of French chefs who rewrote the rules of contemporary cooking in the 1970's: Paul Bocuse; Jacques Pic; Roger Vergé; the Troisgros brothers; Michel Guérard, to name just the best known.

This crew took on the reformist zeal of Fernand Point, and recognised, as the writer Quentin Crewe has pointed out, "that haute cuisine had become so wrapped up in its sauces that the taste of the ingredients was lost, and also that times and customs were changing" This gang, Crewe says, were "the liberation of French cooking from the straitjacket imposed on it at the beginning of the century by Escoffier."

But, 20 years later, Crewe would berate the nouvelle cuisine maestros: "Possibly the worst effect of the general brouhaha was the air of commercialism that spread among grand restaurants. Instead of being shrines of gastronomy... they became big businesses."

The rule here is simple: those who effect dynastic change are also the very people who come to resist their dynasties being changed, but change must occur in cooking.

If the French have been slow to pull down the statues, the Spanish, to take one example, have not hesitated to make it new. Spain, right now, is perhaps the key European destination for

THE WELL-TRAVELLED RESTAURATEUR
shifting • the • zeitgeist

restaurateurs who are open to new ideas.

"The effervescence that buoyed French nouvelle cuisine in the 1970's has somehow been piped across the Pyrenees", wrote Arthur Lubow in a seminal article in the *New York Times Magazine*, and he quotes Charlie Trotter: "Spain is where the zeitgeist has shifted."

Of course, Lubow identifies the extraordinary Ferran Adria of El Bulli as the catalyst of the Spanish "new nouvelle cuisine", but he also identifies one signal aspect of Spain's culinary ascendancy: "Many of these chefs seem like comrades-in-arms, working together to advance their country's cuisines."

So, what addresses should be on the list of the well-travelled restaurateur? Well, the top dozen chefs in Spain, for a start, such as Andoni Luis Aduriz, whose menu from the wildly exciting Mugaritz is quoted in part earlier in this book; Isaac Salaberia of Fagollaga; and the modest Victor Arguinzoniz of Extebarri, are the sort of cooks who, almost instinctively, push the envelope in their own individual way, but they are simply a few of a new group whose work has a missionary zeal.

And, because the older chefs who inspired these men are still at work, it is possible to see and taste the last 30 years of Spanish cooking, from the work of chefs such as Juan Mari Arzak or Pedro Subijana via Martin Berasategui and on into the future.

But whilst Spain appears to present the picture of a culinary culture at a time of excited foment, there are many other great cooks and restaurateurs whose work will serve to inspire the well-travelled restaurateur. The Irish chef and restaurateur Paul Flynn has written brilliantly of his visits to Charlie Trotter's in

Chicago. Heston Blumenthal in The Fat Duck in Berkshire in England is another whose cooking has become a mecca for other chefs.

But chasing culinary superstars isn't the only way to travel. Often, the best lessons are learnt in the simplest possible ways: the lightness of touch that is the signature of Bill Granger's cooking; the correct way to make salt-cured duck, or even the perfect sandwich, which you might eat at Sheridan's Cheesemongers in Galway, that duck and those sandwiches being the work of Dave Gumbleton, who worked with Tetsuya Wakuda for many years. Street food in Bangkok might suddenly illuminate some new way of creating broth, or help you to understand how to use chillies. Often, what you need to know is out there and, often, it is the commonplace thing that is right in front of you.

And, if there is a rule, it is to pay attention to the people who are on the way up: the guys who are chasing the stars, not the guys who already have them. If you hit The French Laundry and Alain Ducasse and Taillevent and Gordon Ramsay and Nobu and Jean-Georges, you will certainly learn a lot and most definitely you will pay a lot. But will you learn just what you need to know?

And don't just pay attention to the cooking: look closely at the rooms, the service, and look closely at the bathrooms. Take the bits of someone else's style and concept that can fit into your own place, and then assimilate them.

If you simply copy them, then you consign yourself to second place. Learning is the synthesis of your own work and that of others, and travelling is the best way to begin that synthesis.

TESTIMONY

Bridget Healy, Café Paradiso, Cork

1 BUSINESS SENSE

Marry a great cook with a good head for business.

2 APPROACH

Try to always find people fascinating, in all their myriad weird shapes and forms, even when they are…err…challenging.

3 PASSION

Maintain a consuming passion for food and wine.

4 RESENTMENT

Don't resent the work - work double shifts when you have to, take a night off when you can - it will all come out in the wash.

5 HOLIDAYS

Try to stick to a five-day week and take regular holiday breaks to refresh your energy and enthusiasm. There's nothing worse than a cranky, bitter restaurant manager.

6 SHARING

Never serve anything to a customer that you wouldn't eat or drink yourself.

7 SMUGNESS

Don't get smug – always keep trying to raise the standards.

8 RELATIONSHIPS

Only employ people and build close business relations with people that you'd want to have round for dinner at your house.

9 EXPECT THE BEST

Expect the best from everyone – mostly, you'll get it.

10 GIVE THANKS

Give thanks every day that you have such a great job, and that you'll never have to go back to that awful office if you keep working hard.

11 CLEANING

Never expect anyone to do anything you wouldn't do yourself, whether it be reaching for high standards or cleaning behind the toilets.

12 PLUMBING

Learn plumbing, carpentry and minor electrical work.

primer

• **Restaurateurs must travel in order to learn from and assimilate the examples of chefs in other culinary cultures.**

• **Chefs who argue about the merits of tradition over innovation are missing the point: cooking must always evolve, change, adapt and be made new. Otherwise it simply dies.**

• **Don't confine your culinary travels to visiting expensive gastronomic temples. Often the most important lessons are to be learnt in the simplest, most obvious places.**

• **When you are travelling, don't just pay attention to the food. Look at all the elements of the restaurant and take whatever lessons you can from the total experience.**

• **The people to pay attention to are the guys who are on their way up the ladder of recognition, not those with the stars and the reputations.**

13

13

"Awareness, paying attention,
noticing is the first and most important
step to enjoying food."

DENIS COTTER

PARADISO REGAINED

There will be many restaurateurs, and wanna-be restaurateurs, who will have reached this concluding stage of the book, and who will be tearing their hair out with frustration.

"Why all this airy-fairy stuff?" they will be asking. "Why not the nuts and bolts of the business. The Who? The Where? The When? The Why? The How Much?"

Why not, indeed. The answer is because the nuts and bolts are necessary to get your doors open, but they are not the things that bring in the customers. What I have learnt, as a critic and as a consultant, not to mention my many years as a dishwasher, is that it is all that other stuff that makes a restaurant succeed.

You can reduce the act of cooking food, serving food and eating food to a matter of mechanics, and what you wind up with is a fast-food restaurant.

I spent a year working in a fast food restaurant, and it was a depressing, and ultimately valuable, experience, because it taught me that fast food joints are actually the inverse of restaurants. They are places where the elements that make eating a cultural experience, all the things that give food and the culture of food a genuine meaning, have been emptied out. They are culinary and cultural black holes: places without the very essence of life, places where the very aspects of civilisation which we can attach to eating are not just deracinated, but banished entirely.

So, of course the mechanics of the trade are important to running a business successfully – you have to do the VAT and write the wine list, as the restaurateur's testimonies arrayed throughout this book testify – but unless you can transcend the mechanics of the business, unless you can make your work into a creative and artistic endeavour, unless you can make the entertainment, then you will fail.

Restaurants that succeed, in other words, are transcendent. They lift us up. They take us out of the mundanities of everyday life, and take us into an oasis of civility and calm, a place where service has an emotional engagement between staff and customer, a place of leisure and pleasure.

And this entertainment is, first and foremost, a cultural entertainment. Great restaurants mirror the societies and the individuals that create them. This is the point made, in a typically modest way, by Cork chef Denis Cotter in his two classic books, *The Café Paradiso Cookbook* and *Paradiso Seasons*.

Read Cotter's thoughts on the business of running a restaurant, and you come face to face with someone whose engagement with the culture has come from a series of profound shocks, the sort of intellectual and cultural dilemmas that lead to, in Cotter's case, a very profound simplicity.

"A cook's job is to get the food to the customers with these qualities intact", is how Cotter writes of gathering and preserving the intrinsic nature of the foods he cooks with. This is, of course, the antithesis of the standard view of the chef's job, where the chef sees his aim as being to transform the ingredients, via his skills, into something elaborate.

But Cotter is more modest: he is the servant of the ingredients presented to him by his suppliers, he is part of the cultural chain, the food chain, that stretches from grower to customer via cook. "When the magic works best, the cook is a medium", Cotter writes in *Paradiso Seasons*.

HOW TO RUN A RESTAURANT

PARADISO REGAINED
that • other • stuff

In *The Ballymaloe Cookbook*, Myrtle Allen touches on exactly the same vision: "The butter your sister is sending us is very good", I said to my neighbour one day. "Yes", he said, "that field always made good butter".

This is no more than the famous aphorism of one of the greatest food writers, Curnonsky, which we quoted in the first edition of this book: "La cuisine! That's when things taste like themselves". Famous this quote may be, but it is also famously ignored by chefs throughout the world.

In *Paradiso Seasons*, Cotter develops the point: "Clever cooking applied to poor ingredients often makes for depressing eating, a point which is often lost on expensive restaurants."

I like the way in which Denis Cotter, talking about the seasonality of foods, tells us that "it is crucial to recognise the hero of the season." Why should restaurants be obsessive about seasonality? Because in world of increasingly processed and globalised foods, it gives you a USP: there is precious little seasonality today in the average domestic kitchen.

He returns to this idea in *Paradiso Seasons*: "There is an holistic sense of well-being we enjoy when our hunger is truly satisfied that can only be had from eating good food cooked with great care. We have forgotten that the balance we often have such difficulty maintaining in our relationship with food is present in the natural seasonal order."

Present, and correct.

Denis Cotter may be modest, but he doesn't lack ambition. "The opportunity that exists is, I believe, to accept that we have an almost blank page and to cook as we see fit from the finest produce we can muster."

To put this declaration of intent another way, each artist-cook has a *tabula rasa*: after you have done all the hard work in the business of creating your own signature style, you discover that the slate has been wiped clean, ready for you to make your mark. This is the thrilling possibility of all art: start anew, and make it new.

Cotter develops the theme of the creativity of cooking by telling the story of receiving his first slice of praise, whilst working in his first kitchen in New Zealand: "I swelled to twice my normal operational size for about an hour and a half of heady bliss, then drank far too much Thai whisky and fell asleep. I was honoured and knew how I wanted to cook. This relationship with the people who eat the food is an immeasurably important element in the development of my cooking and the spirit of Café Paradiso."

Here we see the perfect creative relationship at work: the originality of the cook wins praise, and this dynamic and direct relationship creates the spirit of the restaurant, but also serves to keep the chef striving, developing. When I argue that the business of running a restaurant is a creative, artistic calling, it is precisely this relationship and its dynamic that I am talking about, the heady creativity, spontaneity, satisfaction, the appreciation and the acclaim that we saw in the story of Otto Kunze dealt with at the beginning of this book.

Cotter sums it up like this: "I love to work in that area where simple food done unbelievably well bowls people over, though I am old enough to accept that restaurant food needs to have airs of mystery and magic about it too."

In fact, the mystery and the magic are pivotal to the restaurant experience, and you achieve them by tapping into the transcendent ambition I mentioned earlier, that alchemy of human interaction.

In the most recent Bridgestone restaurant guide I have written, I struggled to describe the impact of the last visit I had made to Café Paradiso. All I could come up with was to compare the delirious magic of it to Miles Davis' seminal recording of a series of Chicago gigs, *Live at The Plugged Nickel*, three nights when one of the great Davis groups – Herbie Hancock, Wayne Shorter, Ron Carter and Tony Williams playing with Miles – simply tore the rule book apart.

They were able to tear the book apart because of individual skill, but above this it was the level of mutuality and sympathy that was transcendent. Individually, but more especially together, they were out-of-the-box, on-top-of-their-game.

Cotter's crew in Café Paradiso did just the same thing: in a restaurant space that is much like any other, they created a restaurant experience that was unlike any other. It wasn't just a restaurant experience: it was an artistic experience. That is the magic at work, the sinuous improvising-in-time that great restaurants can achieve.

"RUNNING A RESTAURANT IS NO JOKE, SO I ALWAYS TRY TO SEE THE LIGHTER SIDE OF THINGS"

PAUL FLYNN

Jonathan Davis, Alden's Restaurant, Belfast

WHAT MAKES A RESTAURANT SUCCESSFUL?

The million-dollar question.

I am always reminded of the American Express advert where the owner of yo-sushi! says "if anyone ever looked at the success rate for restaurants no one would ever open a restaurant." He however is a living testimony of what can be achieved.

When Alden's first opened just over five year's ago, people questioned why we opened in a residential neighbourhood of Belfast rather than the city centre (still repeated to this day in some of the guide books, Bridgestone excluded).

Nowadays the regular customers do not bat an eyelid and some even believe it was a shrewd choice as we have a monopoly position with all the "chimney pots" in the area.

People's views change over time; changed I believe by what you give your customer day in and day out. It may take time to notice but attitudes will change for the better or for the worse.

WHAT IS MOST IMPORTANT TO BE SUCCESSFUL?

• A passion for what you are doing.

• Getting and keeping the right staff.

• Key staff singing from the same hymn sheet.

• Getting margins right on your total sales.

• Building a relationship with your customers and honestly listening to what they have to say.

• Not changing for the sake of change but with the aim of continual improvement.

• Not just being interested in one facet of the business. As Cath (the head chef) still tries to teach me, look at everything not just your balance sheet or your food - everything counts. Keeping your window ledges clean, staff uniform, and toilet soap are as important as everything else is.

• Patience (I'm still waiting!)

14

14

"I think that cooking
is a question of emotion."

FERRAN ADRIA

MAKE IT BEAUTIFUL
care • care • care

"RESPECT FOR FOOD IS ONE OF THE MOST IMPORTANT THINGS TO HAVE, EVEN IF IT'S FOR THE HUMBLEST OF VEGETABLES."

RICHARD CORRIGAN

Great restaurateurs make eating in restaurants an aesthetic experience, and they create this aesthetic through care.

Care, paying attention to detail, is the secret to making something beautiful, from that coffee-to-go through to the grandest multi-course celebration dinner. Taking care and showing care, makes things beautiful and it makes things work.

Care shows in the gleam of the glasses and the mirrors.

It shows in the sharpness and cut of the uniforms of the staff, and the crunchy chewyness of the bread rolls. It shows in the choice of music, and the choice of paintings. It shows in the language and politesse of the staff.

It shows in the food, right down to the smallest detail of the presentation: the pat of butter, the bowl of porridge, the texture of the scrambled eggs or the crab risotto, the slow-roasted shank of lamb or the fresh pasta. Even before the food appears, it shows in the care with which ingredients have been bought, foraged and brought to the restaurant. It shows in how the food is described, in menus that are road maps of the region, and alephs of the entire world of specialist food.

It is apparent from the design of the menu, whether it be scribbled on a blackboard or elegantly designed in a plush folder. Accessible, affordable, tempting, creative, the language of the menu should introduce and entice the customer to the food.

It shows in the choice of wines and the precision and concision of language used to describe them. It shows in how the sommelier opens the bottle and pours the tasting soupçon.

Care shows in the emotional engagement of the service, that vital link between cook and customer.

Care makes everything beautiful. It also makes working in a restaurant a pleasure, despite the pressures, despite the improvising in time, despite the clamour and mayhem that are normal life in the business.

Care makes money, curiously enough. Because it brings people back to the restaurant time after time, because it is the element that creates loyal and regular customers, it is the one element that will ensure that the bottom line looks after itself.

Care creates that community of producers, cooks and customers that can grace any country with a meaningful, creative, dynamic food culture.

It is care that makes the magic that we experience when a restaurant experience is at its height.

"THERE IS SOMETHING ETERNALLY APPEALING ABOUT THE IDEA OF A RESTAURANT..."

TERENCE CONRAN

"IF I COULD START A FASHION,
IT WOULD BE TO RECAPTURE SOME
FORGOTTEN FLAVOURS,
OR TO PRESERVE SOME THAT MAY
SOON DIE."

MYRTLE ALLEN

"GOOD HONEST FOOD PRODUCED
WITH PASSION AND ATTENTION TO
DETAIL."

SIMON PRATT

"I THINK THAT COOKING IS A
QUESTION OF EMOTION,
AND NOT A COMPETITION."

FERRAN ADRIA

"ALL RESTAURATEURS ARE AN UNCOMFORTABLE MIXTURE OF SERVANT AND PARENT."

A.A. GILL

"THE TRUE MEASURE OF SERVICE IS THE LEVEL OF HONEST HOSPITALITY AND VALUE BEING OFFERED."

DANNY MEYER

"SIMPLICITY MEANS TAKING RAW FOOD, UNDERSTANDING IT AND COOKING IT VERY LITTLE. YOU COOK FOOD TO KEEP THE FLAVOURS, FOR ALL THE FLAVOURS ARE THERE."

NOEL McMEEL

BIBLIOGRAPHY

• **Conran, Terence.** *On Restaurants*. Conran Octopus, London, 2000.

• **Cotter, Denis.** *The Cafe Paradiso Cookbook*; *Paradiso Seasons*.
Atrium, Cork, 1999, 2003.

• **Flynn, Paul.** *An Irish Adventure with Food*. Collins Press, Cork, 2003.

• **Gill, A.A.** *The Ivy, The Restaurant & Its Recipes*. Hodder & Stoughton, London, 1997.

• **Granger, Bill.** *Sydney Food; Bill's Food; Bill's Open Kitchen*. Murdoch Books,
Sydney, 2001-2003.

• **Hill, Shaun.** *Cooking at The Merchant House*. Conran Octopus, London, 2000.

• **Keller, Thomas.** *The French Laundry Cookbook*. Artisan, New York, 1999.

• **Lawler, Edmund.** *Lessons in Service from Charlie Trotter.* Ten Speed, Berkeley, 2001.

• **Meyer, Danny and Romano, Michael.** *The Union Square Café Cookbook*.
Harper Collins, New York, 1994.

• **McKenna, John.** *How to Run a Restaurant*. Estragon Press, Durrus, 1998.

• **Molyneux, Joyce.** *The Carved Angel Cookery Book*. Collins, London, 1990.

• **Symons, Michael.** *A History of Cooks and Cooking*. Prospect Books, Devon, 2001.

• **Tower, Jeremiah.** *California Dish*. Free Press, California, 2003.

INDEX

INDEX

INDEX

INDEX

last forever, that they come and go. It's the same with the bad times. They come and go, too.

The trick is to get into the habit of reminding ourselves that everything – good and bad – is temporary. So when you're in that valley, keep giving yourself that message. *It's temporary*. Write it down. Stick it on your desk, on the mirror in the bathroom, the bedside table, anywhere you're going to see it, and keep repeating it; *it's temporary*.

In time, the bad things don't even get to you in the way they once did because you see them for what they are – events that will pass.

It's Your Life

Every day we're learning how to manage our emotions and not to let them dominate. That doesn't mean getting rid of negative feelings – it means handling them in the right way. The only way to be in control and free is not to be ruled by your emotional state and it's a balancing act – a question of finding the means to control your emotions without being a cold person. If you can control your emotional state, you'll be controlled in the way you treat yourself and other people.

Everything we do expresses what kind of a person we are. If someone goes into your kitchen to make a cup of tea and they leave the spoon on the floor, the tea bag dripping all over the counter, don't bother putting the milk back in the fridge, what does that tell you? It tells me that person is all over the place emotionally, that they don't know what they're doing, they're a mess, a walking disaster. It's about discipline and it filters down to every aspect of your being. When you're not in control of your emotions, believe me, your life has no order.

Until you control your emotional state, you'll find the same things keep coming up over and over. It's like the movie, *Groundhog Day*. The same stuff every day until you wake up to what's really going on.

Life is what *you* create and *you* have the power to change it any choose. Remember, it's your movie. You're in charge. You don't like again. No one else can do it. There's no sense sitting around waiting guru to come along and give you the answers. You have to do it, go h yourself, do the work, create the answers, be your own guru. You can't slump in front of the telly night after night hoping the life you want is to appear by magic, without you having to do anything.

Get cracking.
- Don't just sit there – do something.
- Bring about change, one step at a time.
- Be in control of your destiny.

Self-awareness gives you the knowledge and the means to make positi changes. No one is stuck with a life they don't want. The life you're livin right now is the one you've chosen. If your home's chaotic, your relationship are always a mess, your job is making you stressed, you're eating and drinking too much and hating yourself for it, it's not because life's unfair – it's because you're not fulfilling your potential. You're not doing the work.

We *all* have freedom and choice. What we do with it really is up to us.

Change for the Better

Becoming more self-aware means your perception starts to change. Life looks different. It feels different. It is different. Once you're disciplined about leading a life that's ethical, caring and spiritual, balancing being selfless with self-care, you find that the negative stuff – obsessive behaviour, eating disorders, destructive addictions – has no power over you. You still hear the old man in the rocking chair, but he has a lot less to say and he's not controlling you anymore. You don't even listen to him most of the time.

spiritually that stops me falling apart. That's really
what keeps me going above all else. Maybe you're
not convinced. You can't see the point in praying.
You think you know people who have no
spiritual connection and still manage to do all
right. I'd like to see those people because there's
something you're not seeing. I really believe our
connection with some kind of Higher Power is
crucial and that when that's the focus of your life
everything else, all the things you're struggling with, start to make sense.

> When you have a spiritual relationship your life changes

I believe we are all much more than skin and bone and that until you connect
with your spirit you'll never fulfil your true potential. It's like trying to do a
complicated mathematical puzzle when you don't have all the numbers you need.
The spirit is a massive part of the equation and there's no peace without it.

No bling bling, no fancy car, no big house, no amount of money in the
bank is going to give you peace, it doesn't matter who you are. When you
have a spiritual relationship your life changes. The things that tripped you up
before cease to be a problem. You have a different perspective. The bad habits
you couldn't manage to break start to lose their grip. You know toxicity when
you see it and you just don't go there.

The work you do every day on awareness, having a purpose in life, makes
you more compassionate, more tolerant, more loving and forgiving – and
that makes you a more spiritual being.

When you make the spiritual element the number one priority in your life
it all falls into place. There's no load to carry. The peace you feel inside is
reflected in your physical well-being. You look better than ever. I see it
working for me every day and I sometimes think – 'Oh man, if I'd known it
was this good I'd have gone there ages ago.'

My strict religious upbringing gave me a belief system, faith in God and
the power of prayer, a sound moral and ethical code and I'll always be grateful
for that. Now, though, my church is inside me, and the daily work I do on
my self-awareness is my religion.

Heaven on Earth

I've realised there are only two ways in life – you either want to die or you want to live. It's a simple, stark choice. One or the other. I want to live my life to the full, experience heaven right here on earth – and I want to encourage other women to do the same.

I'm now in a good place with my life. I've got two beautiful children, a good relationship with myself, a great relationship with the universe, and a real sense of purpose, but I know I still have a long way to go.

The more I do, the more I want to do. I don't want to waste a single moment, to feel I'm not making the most of my time on this planet, and that's what gives me a sense of urgency and makes me so driven.

I'm on a mission to inspire women to realise their potential rather than settle for a life that's frustrating and unfulfilling.

The world we live in is one of infinite possibilities. We just have to trust they're there and go looking for them, focus only on the positive, not let life's knocks make us cynical.

The work never stops, but the more you do, the easier it gets, and the knocks start to feel more like grazes, nothing to get worked up about.

I think we're all in a race, all at different stages, some people in front, some behind, and some right alongside us. There are plenty of people ahead of me and that's fine. I slip up, fall behind, and that's also fine. I don't set myself up as someone who knows it all – just a runner in the race who's playing it straight every step of the way.

All I'm advocating is an honest way of living that benefits you and the world around you. It's about living by your truth, not by anyone else's, and having faith in the spiritual side of yourself, which takes courage because it means putting your trust in something you can't see or explain.

The minute the universe sees you trust it, it's like something clicks into place. Suddenly the lights go on and the glow that gives you inside shows on the outside. The world becomes a different place and you become a different person.

You look amazing, you don't age, people start asking what's going on with you because you don't look like the same person anymore. They see the confidence, the fearlessness, the love of life you have, and they want to be part of it. That's when people find you attractive and want to be around you. It has nothing to do with being thin or looking like a model or having a nose job or being the most beautiful woman in the world – it's much more about what's going on *inside*. It's about the aura that's coming off you.

People keep telling me I look like I'm 25, which feels crazy when I know I'm 37. They see me with my 15-year-old daughter and think she's my mate. What I've noticed is the more work I do on myself, the less obsessed I am about the way I look. It's not the focus of my attention the way it used to be. Don't get me wrong, I put my make-up on for work, make an effort to look nice and take a pride in my appearance, but then I forget all about it because there are other, more interesting things going on. Focusing too much on physical appearance becomes petty compared with all the other stuff in life. When your

We all have the power to create the life we choose

focus is about *feeling* good, *being* good, and *doing* good, you no longer need to obsess about looking good because it comes with the territory anyway.

I think the tide is turning, that society's obsession with women starving themselves to conform to an unhealthy ideal of beauty, being fearful of ageing, resorting to cosmetic surgery through insecurity and low self-worth, can't last. I really believe it's inevitable that all these pressures will implode at some point because they're built on stuff that isn't all that important.

And, more and more, women will realise there are ways of looking great, feeling good in their skin, and having fulfilling lives that don't crush their femininity.

We all have the power to create the life we choose. No one is stuck. Nobody has to settle for less than they want. That's the beauty of the universe we live in. You just have to *want* to change your reality, *believe* you can do it, and be prepared to put the *work* in. That's all there is to it.

The moment you start to change the way you think, you're on your way to having the life you want. We're all mini-gods, capable of great things, it's just we're not taught to think like that, and that's why we have to encourage each other.

I know how much my own life has changed, that it gets better every day, that my emotional, physical and spiritual health is stronger than ever, and that I'm constantly amazed by the opportunities that come my way.

Every day I feel like I'm another step closer to having heaven on earth and that the great stuff just keeps on coming. It's there for any woman serious about change, committed to well-being and passionate about life.

What's stopping you?

Index